Insurance

How the Wealthy Use Life Insurance as a Tax-free Personal Bank

(Discover How to Start and Sustain a Successful Career Selling Insurance)

David Smalley

Published By **Phil Dawson**

David Smalley

All Rights Reserved

Insurance: How the Wealthy Use Life Insurance as a Tax-free Personal Bank (Discover How to Start and Sustain a Successful Career Selling Insurance)

ISBN 978-0-9948647-8-9

No part of this guidebook shall be reproduced in any form without permission in writing from the publisher except in the case of brief quotations embodied in critical articles or reviews.

Legal & Disclaimer

The information contained in this book is not designed to replace or take the place of any form of medicine or professional medical advice. The information in this book has been provided for educational & entertainment purposes only.

The information contained in this book has been compiled from sources deemed reliable, and it is accurate to the best of the Author's knowledge; however, the Author cannot guarantee its accuracy and validity and cannot be held liable for any errors or omissions. Changes are periodically made to this book. You must consult your doctor or get professional medical advice before using any of the suggested remedies, techniques, or information in this book.

Upon using the information contained in this book, you agree to hold harmless the Author from and against any damages, costs, and expenses, including any legal fees potentially resulting from the application of any of the information provided by this guide. This disclaimer applies to any damages or injury caused by the use and application, whether directly or indirectly, of any advice or information presented, whether for breach of contract, tort, negligence, personal injury, criminal intent, or under any other cause of action.

You agree to accept all risks of using the information presented inside this book. You need to consult a professional medical practitioner in order to ensure you are both able and healthy enough to participate in this program.

Table Of Contents

Chapter 1: The Definitive Guide To Buying Burial Insurance 1

Chapter 2: Expert Advice For Consumers On Final Expense Whole Life Insurance.. 22

Chapter 3: Six Steps To Buying The Best Final Expense Insurance Policy 57

Chapter 4: Mini Topics Related To Final Expense Insurance 72

Chapter 5: Best Burial Insurance For Memory Disorders 85

Chapter 6: Best Burial Insurance For Cancer History 87

Chapter 7: Best Burial Insurance For Depression, Bipolar, And Schizophrenia. 90

Chapter 8: Best Burial Insurance For Cardiac Issues 93

Chapter 9: Best Burial Insurance For Diabetes.. 103

Chapter 10: Best Burial Insurance For Kidney Issues 107

Chapter 11: Best Burial Insurance For Hiv 114

Chapter 12: Best Burial Insurance For Smokers 122

Chapter 13: What Is The History Of Insurance? 127

Chapter 14: What Is Life Insurance? 139

Chapter 15: What Is Health Insurance? 147

Chapter 16: What Exactly Does Home Insurance Cover? 158

Chapter 17: Why Do I Require Renter's Insurance? 168

Chapter 18: Where Do I Buy Car Insurance? 181

Chapter 1: The Definitive Guide To Buying Burial Insurance

As an expert in the field of burial insurance many people ask, "What is the BEST kind of burial life insurance?"

This is a good concern. More likely than not it is the case that you are presented with a myriad of choices to purchase burial insurance for senior citizens each and every day. There are, for instance, many advertisements in the news for Colonial Penn, MetLife, Mutual of Omaha, and Physicians Mutual. Also, don't forget the spam mail is sent out daily by various funeral insurance firms.

There are times when so many choices, it's quite confusing and could make people who truly require a burial insurance plan to do nothing whatsoever.

In the next post, I'll discuss in detail the various ways to get burial insurance. The goal of course is to provide you with the maximum amount of information on how various final cost burial insurance policies operate and the best way to determine which options you have in terms of burial life insurance.

Term Life Burial Insurance

The initial burial insurance option for senior citizens I'll go over is what's referred to by the term "term life" insurance. You may have received mailings coming from AARP and Globe Life Insurance. When you read the mailers they write, usually you'll see that they will only provide coverage for that extends to but not more than a specific age the near future. What we mean by this is "terminating," or term or insurance. The word that is most important is TERMINATING.

What's wrong in Life insurance for term?

In the first place, terms life insurance policies for expenses at the end of your life don't match up with the main reason why people purchase funeral insurance for senior citizens. The truth is that the principal reason to purchase the burial insurance policy is to ensure the death benefit no whatever age you die.

The reason why you require your burial insurance death benefits guarantee? Because death can be unpredictable! You WILL die, guaranteed!

So, the idea of the term life insurance policy for burial insurance poses to ask,

"Why take the risk of not having coverage when you need it?"

How A Term Life Insurance Policy For A Senior Went From $50 To $350 A Month!

A few years ago, when I was a brand new funeral insurance agent I was introduced to a lovely 82 year old lady. She was a cleaner throughout her life, and she was working for 20 hours every week, dry-cleaning. Her overall health was excellent and she was in good health.

In relation to her burial insurance her plan was that was offered by a well-known firm. The plan she chose included a term insurance program. While the plan did not end until she was 90, her cost of the term insurance increased each year during the past 12 years.

It was initially $50 per month for term insurance is now at 350 dollars a month. However, she was able to afford the cost because she was working part-time and was able to draw Social Security.

How Burial Life Insurance Can Become Unaffordable Overnight

Her health was deteriorating and her condition took an unexpected turn for the worse. The doctor advised open heart surgery in order for removing an obstruction. As she turned 82 when she was diagnosed, she was ordered to go into retirement.

As she had lost the income from her job as a part-time worker She was placed in a tight spot. There were bills to pay and she had not enough money to pay the cost of a $350 premium for term insurance. In addition to the damage, she had the option an insurance replacement for her term policy in a matter of minutes by a burial insurance policy. Because of her open heart procedure, her sole choice was a two-year time period for burial insurance (which I will explain in greater depth in the coming days).

This tragic story is a daily occurrence. Many people do an excellent job in having a burial insurance policy set up. But, they aren't sure the way it functions. Most of the time, it's because the funeral insurance representative didn't clarify it. In addition, the person could have intentionally concealed information from the insured.

As she is well into retirement she doesn't have the money for costly term life insurance or even the health that would qualify to receive a higher premium. No matter what you do, don't make the same mistake as this lady.

Permanent Burial Insurance Policy Options

In the case of burial insurance for seniors The opposite of a term insurance plan is a long-term policy. Permanent burial insurance will last until you have paid the cost. Through the rest of your life regardless of how long you live you will be covered with a guarantee for a certain funeral benefit to your beneficiary of option.

As I do, funeral agents typically suggest permanent burial insurance for older people seeking the final cost coverage. Why? The reason is that the form of the policy conforms to what is actually happening.

Guarantees In Your Burial Insurance Policy

Like we said earlier that a burial insurance policy which does not cover you beyond an age limit doesn't serve you well. If you have a perpetual burial insurance plan, as long as you're paying the premium, you'll have insurance. It's unlikely that you'll be facing a scenario where you will outlive the policy! In the event that you pass away and the policy's premiums are up to date and the policy will pay the death benefit according to instructions by the policy.

In the realm of the permanent insurance, you have many possibilities. It is your goal to discover the policy that you or your loved ones (if you're spouse or children looking for funeral insurance on the parent) are eligible for.

Following is a brief overview of various options available that provide permanent insurance.

Guaranteed Acceptance Burial Insurance Policy

In the first place, you are guaranteed acceptance of your whole life insurance.

A guarantee of acceptance means that the insurance policy can be offered in all circumstances regardless of the state of health. If you are older than the age limit it is impossible for the business to reject the policy. If you're able to feel a pulse, and are able to sign your name on the record, you'll be approved. This policy is an excellent alternative for those who are otherwise insurable, for example people with Alzheimer's disease, currently diagnosed cancer (those who have not had cancer for a long time have more alternatives) or kidney dialysis.

You can see, there are disadvantages. Let me explain. In general, a guarantee issue burial insurance policy gives the first day 100% complete insurance for accidental deaths just. Accidental deaths cannot be fully insured for a two minimum years.

This is the reality. Many seniors die of nature-based causes, they are not a result of accident. Thus If the guaranteed acceptance burial insurance policy for seniors is your sole choice, you will not have insurance for natural deaths until 2 years from the date of effective in the plan.

Why Would One Get A Guaranteed Issue Burial Life Insurance Policy?

The reason you should purchase the guaranteed issue insurance is the fact that you've looked at other options before. The person has tried to find complete coverage in other ways but have been denied the coverage. Thus, a guarantee acceptance life insurance policy should be the only option you can consider.

The main issue with life insurance that is no-questions-asked is that it is often offered to the general public as the primary option to cover burial costs! It is shocking to realize that the majority of choices available in burial insurance is assured acceptance insurance.

It is a good idea to speak about burial life insurance with an agent who may offer the possibility of providing you with complete first-day coverage or even partial coverage for the first day. Why? Because death can be a bit uncertain. While many believe that we'll live for an extended time, everyone knows that it will be impossible to know the end day. The time we have is short. We're not sure when it'll be and need to prepare for it that's why we have the second option - the burial insurance that is full coverage for senior citizens.

Burial Insurance With Whole Life

The best scenario is to get an all-day, fully-covered burial insurance life-insurance policy. This isn't an easy process.

But, not all burial insurance choices are created equal. Let's take it further and discuss the differences when the use of a broker and the captive agent.

Captive Agents

If you're obligated to one particular insurance agency or company, you're an "captive" agent. In the realm of burial insurance, a captive agent generally represents one business. Because captive agents' choices can only be limited to one firm and they can only provide only one option for coverage for you, the customer.

While that might sound great, the reality is that one choice generally is not the best alternative for the vast majority of individuals!

If collaborating with an agent captive is not the best choice for you then what else is?

Independent Agents

You'd like to partner with a person who gives many options when it comes to funeral life insurance. Why? because by having a captive agent you are either losing regarding coverage quality or the price.

We can compare the cost of burial insurance with purchasing food items. When you're ready to shop do you want to go to the store which only stocks only one kind of animal, one variety of bread, or a specific type of vegetable? Would you prefer to shop at a place offering a range of alternatives in food and beverages at lower prices?

The same applies to burial insurance. If the agent you work with only provides the same type of insurance and you're not sure if it's the right one, you'll be paying a higher price to get lesser protection. However, if you were working with an independent agency and had a the best chance to get the most optimal combination of price and quality for burial insurance.

How to Get Low-price, High-quality Burial Insurance

What is the best solution? One option is working in partnership with an independent insurance agent. A person who is independent who can provide the highest quality burial insurance policies. The term "best" defined as a wide range of products that are priced competitively which offer flexibility in underwriting. A person who is an independent agent who isn't tied to just one insurance company. They collaborate with several funeral insurance firms. The company takes the clients desires and needs into account when advising them on the best burial insurance plan.

A lot of times, someone using an independent burial life insurance provider will obtain greater coverage, and will get hundreds of dollars in savings every per year! Additionally funeral insurance typically covers issues an agent who is captive would not provide coverage for.

As an example, the most common conditions that are covered by an insurance company that is independent of a burial broker can include ailments like COPD or heart problems and diabetes, cancer liver and kidney issues neurologic issues, as well as mental health concerns. In many instances captive insurance agents are able to only provide high-priced, assurance of acceptance. But, an independent agent could provide you with complete coverage on the first day!

If you are deciding that burial insurance with whole life coverage is the best option for you, then find an independent agency that shops all the top companies to help you find the most affordable cost and insurance coverage.

Other Burial Insurance For Seniors Options

There are other alternatives to purchase burial insurance for senior citizens Beyond term life insurance, as well as whole life choices. Check out the following article for additional information about other burial insurance plans that are primarily designed for fit applicants and with the financial resources to cover higher costs.

Pre-need Burial Insurance Policy

First, there is the option of pre-need insurance coverage.

Pre-need insurance refers to the burial insurance policy that is that is purchased from a funeral house. Pre-need insurance policies are distinct from burial policies. In the first place, they can be designed to secure your prices for all things that go with the funeral. The cost of your casket, the cost of cremation and the ceremony itself and so on. are secured and backed by insurance.

Also, the policy is one that is paid up. The policy is paid up for 5-10 years prior to paying it off in full. If you die before you pay the entire policy typically, the policy will provide the death benefit in order to pay the funeral expenses when you die. When you purchase pre-need burial assurance policies they work as a type of insurance policy with the additional benefit of helping to reduce the increasing cost of funerals.

The benefit of having for a pre-need funeral insurance policy is that the cost of your insurance will be paid off, and then you'll be able to pay for the funeral entirely. Most people select three to five years payout plan. But, those who are more financially limited choose 7to 10 year payoff plans.

Pre-need Life Insurance Can Be Very Expensive!

The disadvantages of pre-need insurance plans include that they can be three times more expensive. Although many prefer these policies, they can't easily afford it.

And to make things worse If the premiums made to pre-need policies are added together and the sum is greater than what is actually the cost to pay for the funeral.

I've observed many pre-need policy with premiums that is more than double the price of the funeral. There are cases where the cost for the funeral was around $8000 to $10,000 however the actual cost of premiums into was between $15,000 and $20,000.

My opinion is that this plan is not suitable for the majority of. Sure, fighting inflation is a good thing. It's just not worth what is currently being charged for funeral services to ensure that. It's not my opinion!

The cost of funerals has been fairly stable since I started working in the industry since 2011. In the situation, I wouldn't think of pre-need insurance as an option, except if you can pay for it in five years or lesser. If you're at that level it is clear that the costs paid are much more reasonable.

The main benefit of the pre-need insurance plan is that it pays to. You are able to access the same option to pay up with funeral life insurance. In many instances, the cost of the burial insurance plan that you pay for is significantly less. In addition, the underwriting of funeral insurance for older people can be more flexible than the pre-need insurance policies. Consider hiring an independent burial insurance broker if you are a fan of paying-up.

Guaranteed Universal Life For Burial Insurance

Are you healthy and are interested in burial insurance policies with sizes that go that exceed $25,000 in coverage? Think about a guaranteed universal life insurance policy.

The concept behind a guarantee universal insurance plan is comparable as a burial insurance complete life insurance policy. The main distinction is the lack of access to cash. This is because the guaranteed universal life insurance increases the death benefits that are due. As a result, you get the ability to access cash values with a restricted amount.

I would only suggest the guaranteed universal life insurance only if one is seeking an extensive amount of protection. Also, the applicant must be healthy and in good shape. It is less stricer to underwrite and applicants need to be able to comprehend the absence of cash value access for the long-term.

However, guaranteed universal life insurance plans are excellent to those looking for an enormous death benefit.

Summary On Burial Insurance Options

Then you have to ask yourself, which is the most effective option to take?

The first step is to analyze the requirements you have. In other words, what exactly do you intend to achieve with the burial insurance plan?

Perhaps you only want sufficient coverage to cover your funeral. Perhaps you do not wish to leave a lasting inheritance to your grandson or child. Additionally, you might want to give a generous funeral benefit that will replace the income of your family. Find out what your own personal objectives are and then choose the funeral policy one that is most suitable for your needs.

In the majority of people I work with most people, a burial insurance total life insurance product is the most suitable protection option. Why? Burial insurance is a whole-life policy that combines easy underwriting with competitive pricing. It also provides long-term coverage that is not subject to any future rate hikes.

It is best to work in conjunction with an independent insurance agent for the greatest chance of getting first-day all-inclusive coverage. If you are just obtaining guaranteed acceptance life insurance ensure that your agent is shopping different businesses. However, if they don't only offer what is the guaranteed issue burial insurance plan, take into consideration keeping the plan.

Chapter 2: Expert Advice For Consumers On Final Expense Whole Life Insurance

What Is Final Expense Whole Life Insurance?

Whole life insurance with final expense can be described as life insurance to pay for the costs associated with funerals, burials, as well as funeral expenses. Funeral expenses can include items including the casket the urn, and plot. The additional expenses comprise the ceremony costs, the delivery fee, flowers, and so on.

Do you know if there is enough funds to pay for the above-mentioned cost? If yes, then the final cost whole life insurance might be worthwhile to consider.

Hundreds of thousands own a last expense life insurance plan that covers the costs. Why? They're not certain they're able to cover the cost of a purchase on demand out of pocket. Insufficient savings for unexpected circumstances like the death of a loved one is an important reason for people to buy it to begin with.

Most of the time, last expense life insurance plans provide lower mortality benefits. A majority don't opt for a million-dollar final expense policy. Although it's possible to get carried out, most people opt for a policy that's sufficient to pay the cost of a funeral. In general, a plan ranging from the range of $10,000 and $25,000 is typical.

Whole life insurance at final cost policies may be less to less than $10,000. I've assisted clients with plans of $2,000 or $3,000 as all it takes is a simple cremation.

The majority of final expense life insurance policies are the type of insurance that is called simplified issue. They don't require any examinations or physicals. Just fill out the application form, and that's all there is to it! But, there will be times that you need to conduct an interview over the phone to determine the health of you prior to approving.

In the case of final expense, whole life insurance policies there is a chance that you qualify or you do not. Interviews on the phone, which generally take only 10 minutes let us know immediately if you've been approved. It's a quick "yes or no" decision and that's all is needed in the industry.

Why Get A Final Expense Whole Life Insurance Program?

What is the reason to purchase final expense life insurance? Let's look at four primary motives why you should buy a funeral insurance policy.

1. Funeral Costs

The primary reason for purchasing total expense insurance is to remove anxiety about not being able to afford the money needed for funeral costs. The reason is 80-

90% of reasons that people buy a last cost plan.

I'll put it in plain English. Do you worry that if you pass away the family members or spouse will not have enough funds to cover your funeral expenses? If so, a funeral cost whole life insurance policy could be worth looking into.

The majority of those who take out an end-of-life whole life insurance policy are living on fixed income. They've retired. But did you know? They're not wealthy!

While they might be able to retire, the amount is insignificant. The amount they've got in savings doesn't look great too.

In light of the previous, those who purchase final expense life insurance know that death is not predictable. This happens frequently quickly. It's hard to find the time to accumulate enough cash to cover funeral costs.

2. Income Replacement

Another reason for buying the whole life last expense insurance is to protect yourself from having a spouse who earns lesser. In simple terms, you're concerned that the income of your spouse will decrease their lifestyle.

Being an insurance broker who offers final expense life insurance aid those who have these issues often. Imagine your family members having little money left to live off. Does it significantly affect her lifestyle?

Perhaps she isn't able to enjoy the things she's used to. Perhaps she's required to alter her medical insurance. Maybe she's not able to access the medication she requires since the funds aren't available.

If you're worried that your passing could have a profound impact on the lives of your loved ones, an expense-based plan for the future is the ideal solution.

For example I know of a man who was 85 years old when he bought $125,000 of insurance. Although this is an unusually high amount, he also wanted to be able in order to provide a source of income to his wife.

The death occurred after six months. All the insurance policies were have been paid! This made a huge change in the life of his wife because of the importance the feeling of having final expense total life insurance.

3. Non-funeral Related Costs

The 3rd reason why people have the final expense life insurance is that it helps relieve the financial burden caused by "what-ifs" from spouse and relatives.

For the final costs that do not involve funerals there are many things that can take place. There may be savings available right now. There could be an event that requires you need to use your savings.

This is an excellent illustration. I met an ex-police agent in Alabama some time ago. He enjoyed a wonderful pension and lots of money put aside. His wife in retirement as a teacher.

However, the daughter of his father got in the wrong group and began to become addicted to the drugs. If you've read anything about addiction, it's expensive to deal with.

His daughter was only in her 20s at the time this occurred and was at the height of his departure of the force. He used all his savings to get her from jail and fund her rehab numerous times.

The unplanned tragedy changed his life for the worst. If you'd been asking him before his daughter was born, if the same thing was happening it would not have imagined it.

This is why the man has a last expense full life insurance. He wanted an investment plan for any costs that could occur.

The majority of people purchase these insurance plans in order in order to be safe. This is a valid justification to have a last total life insurance plan with no expense. Why? because nobody knows how things will unfold from day to day. Unexpected events can occur and financial demands typically don't go away. The demands for money increase and grow with age.

4. Leaving A Legacy

Another reason for having an end-of-life whole life insurance policy is the ability to create a legacy.

In the same way that I spoke in my earlier post about my mother her newly constructed roof thanks to the $7000 policy that my grandfather had left. Life insurance policies like these are always a blessing to loved ones during the best timing.

Therefore, if you're caring and caring, and feel the desire in your soul to give it a go then a last expense total life insurance policy can be the best way to do it happen.

"Fun" Facts Of Final Expenses

Let's discuss some funeral costs "fun" facts. I have put "fun" in quotes because it's not fun at funerals! There may be some fun at funerals, but it's not the type of enjoyment I'm looking for!

Another major reason why that people purchase final expense life insurance is to pay for their funeral expenses so that their family won't be left without a funeral.

1. Average National Cost Of Burial Expenses

The year 2014 was the time when it was reported that the National Funeral Directors Association estimated the cost of a funeral for 2014 would cost around $8500. Based on my personal knowledge, I'd say this is a true average.

The survey by the NFDA examined all the costs associated with funerals and cremations (we'll come to the cremation process within a moment). The survey included the costs of transportation, the cost of casket, the flowers as well as everything else that goes with funerals.

2. Cremation Expenses

The national NFDA observed that the median cost for cremation is $6,100. Personally, I think that this figure is a bit exaggerated.

Here's why. It's because the NFDA accounts for the full funeral and the expense of cremation. Like you I've been to a number of cremations that cost in the $3000 range or lower.

If you're slightly awestruck by this amount it's likely to be skeptical!

I'm wondering how the NFDA calculated their numbers. I've only seen one or two cremations which had this much value. The majority are less costly. But, remember that NFDA declares that this is the standard for all of us.

Most people these days get an immediate cremation. There may be one small funeral at the church. My grandfather's funeral was held at the Rotary Club. held his funeral held at the Rotary Club for free. If you're going full-time and perform the ceremony, you'll be paying a cost which is high.

This is the real kicker. We've all had enough time to realize that costs increase as you age. Between 2004 and 2014, which is a period that lasted 10 years. Funeral expenses have increased 28.6 per cent!

The NFDA indicates that the typical funeral costs an approximate $2,000 price rise. What's more, look at the previous 10 years between 1994 and 2004. Then there was another 25percent or more rise!

It's evident that funeral services have experienced huge price hikes. This is just like other industries. It's not getting any more affordable. It's a fact that I've been saying for years and it's not true!

What's the significance of this debate? I hope you'll be able to understand how crucial you should think about the longer term. It is essential to ensure that you have sufficient final expense entire life insurance.

Like I mentioned, $8500 is the cost of living today. However, what will happen with pricing twenty or thirty years?

Final Expense Whole Life Insurance - What NOT To Get

Understanding the options available for your total expense life insurance is vital. It is important not to make a mistake!

I've had the pleasure of meeting more than 3,000 people in 2011 for discussions about the total expense life insurance. I've also worked with the final expense insurance brokers within my company across the country. A majority of the people I meet have fixed incomes. Then they are all drowning in ads in junk mail about the final cost insurance.

I'm unable to even go through a conversation with many of them without seeing an advertisement of funeral cost insurance on the television!

If you're majority of people, with increasing amounts of flyers and advertisements about the coverage for final expenses the recipients receive, they get lost.

What I'm looking to do is to cover the non total expense life insurance. It's crucial to be aware of what is excellent and poor coverage. In the next section, we'll discuss the fundamentals of total expense life insurance.

1. Term Insurance The initial cost insurance policy to avoid is"term life insurance.

This is crucial! If there's anything you learn from this post, it's this "term" is short for expires. In essence, if you purchase term insurance it's a bet that you're bound to pass away before the policy is up!

Did you notice this? Terms plans end after which they cease to exist, and then stop! The majority of major insurance companies that you find in the television and in the mail have only term-only insurance. Many of the time the plans are made to expire at age 80! old!

It's possible to purchase term insurance now, then get an average amount of life and lose insurance. That's crazy!

Then it gets more complicated. You will see your premium rates increase in some plan options. They will increase incrementally every five years. While it might be accessible at 60, how affordable would it become more affordable when you reach 65, then 70 then at 75?

Sometimes, it's not. It's my belief that the majority of individuals end up losing their insurance! Why? It's because they can't pay for it any more. All they've ever paid for it. However, Social Security raises simply can't keep up with increase in premiums.

Many drop the position. You don't would like to find yourself in!

Sad fact - we do not exactly when we'll end our lives. This could happen the next day. or 30 years from now. So, it's important to create a budget that is guaranteed to be paid in any situation.

It's essential to have a plan that is guaranteed to follow, as in the absence of a plan, you're making a gamble. You're gambling!

One benefit of term insurance is that it's less expensive initially. However, you'll receive the price you pay.

In simple terms it this way: you'll pay less in short-term insurance. But you'll have to pay a much more in the future!

If you're on a fixed-income that means you only get one paycheck every month. The check must cover everything. The pennies must be counted. Watch everything you purchase.

Imagine getting an rise for your life insurance policy that will double. The first price was $50. Now it's $100. Would you be able to afford that?

There will be other expenses that rise in cost therefore why should you take that risk when there's no need to? This is the reason I am not a fan of people who are looking for final expense protection by taking out a term policy.

This isn't to say that I'm not against term insurance. It's just based on conditions. Most individuals who are looking for a guarantee whole life insurance policy do not require the term insurance.

2. Universal Life

Included in plans for insurance that are not available for purchase is Universal Life insurance.

Here's what you need to know. The reality is that it's not always of Universal Life is a bad final expense insurance policy. There are certain things to be aware of. Do thorough research prior to you buy.

In some cases universal life insurance can be extremely beneficial. It's sometimes the most effective choice! Sometimes, however, it's not. Let me explain.

Universal life insurance isn't always a final cost whole life insurance. In some cases Universal Life plans can be specifically designed to last up to an age.

Often, they'll run for a period of time, ranging from 80 to 85 or even 90 years old.

Therefore the universal life insurance plans function as a short-term insurance policy. They are limited in protection. If you live beyond this plan, then you'll lose coverage or your cost will increase substantially.

The question to be asked is how you will fare if you get to the age of 100? There will be the final costs! You should seriously think about that you're not getting anything that comes with a lifetime warranty.

Universal life insurance might not come with guaranteed levels of prices. There are Universal Life programs with guaranteed prices, and this is the way you ought to do if you are able to find universal life insurance suitable to your needs in life insurance.

But, certain agents make these plans, so that the cost will rise. It's been seen on the streets working with clients face-to-face. Agents have visited and provided the Universal Life plans, and the customer has accepted it for a long time.

When they reach their 70s, they'll receive the massive letter of price increases. Unfortunately, they aren't able to afford the cost anymore. The are obviously furious! This is because the agent had the idea right from the beginning with a plan that was likely to not succeed.

It would take quite a long time until it was able to happen, but finally it came to pass. This isn't to say that Universal Life is not an alternative in any circumstance. It's just a possibility when it comes to certain conditions.

Make sure you're dealing with a professional who comprehends Universal Life plans, how they function, and the things they're doing to help you. Let them tell you the details of their guarantee prior to you purchase any of the plans.

What Type Of Final Expense Whole Life Insurance You SHOULD Get

The last article discussed what you should not to purchase. We'll now discuss what must have in your complete life-long final expense plan.

Here are some of the fundamentals which should be part of each final expense of a whole life insurance plan. Perhaps you're considering something similar to the whole life insurance, also known as permanent insurance. There are times when it's interchangeable terms. You must ensure that you've got the right elements within your plans to ensure that you're getting the highest overall price.

1. Guaranteed Fixed Premium

The first step is to ensure that you are covered by a permanent premium.

One of the greatest benefits that comes with a complete life plan is the fact that it is a constant cost. There is no need to be concerned about obtaining the dreadful price increase notice five years later.

In addition, what you pay today will be what you'll pay up to the point of death. This is great news for those who has a fixed-income.

There's absolutely no danger of not being able to pay for the cost of a rise. It is possible to count on the cost staying the exact. This insurance is essential in any last expense total life insurance policy.

2. Will Not Cancel

Another benefit of a total expense life insurance policy is that it will not be cancelled due to age, health, or illness.

It's crucial! I train my clients to pair the insurance policy they purchase to the specific issue she's looking to solve. All life insurance solves issues. It is also important to note that there are various problems to solve for various people.

If you're a young person doing well, but you suddenly die, your spouse will be in a tense circumstance of having to take over your earnings. It is crucial to have an emergency plan in this situation.

In this case, the best option is the term insurance. Why? because it's the most affordable method of obtaining insurance. If the person dies prior to the expiration date and his spouse inherits the entire amount I would have made if I been alive.

All of us will pass away. It's a fact that it could occur at any time. It is a fact that certain expenses are likely to be incurred. It is not a good idea to create plans that end before we have time to pay.

Take a moment to think about the issue. What is the rationale behind the logic? Why should I be paying for a policy that I could be able to outlive?

That's why your last total life insurance premium should be guaranteed to not expire due to age or illness.

3. Death Benefits Do Not Decrease

The third goal is to get a guaranteed death benefit which does not diminish.

I've seen decreasing death benefit life insurance plans. As they approach the age of a specific number and their coverage decreases. Yet, they'll remain the same the price!

If you're looking for the final cost of life insurance, the plan you will see is the plan you will receive. It is important to find a plan which covers the entire life of you. You also want plans that don't expire due to age or your health is poor. Furthermore, you would like your plan to be exactly the same from start until the end.

It's quite straightforward. There's nothing complex than that!

4. First-day 100% Coverage

In the end, make an effort to achieve total coverage.

Like I said earlier I mentioned earlier, you're sifting through an abundance of junk mail as well as TV advertisements for last expense total life insurance advertising. However, the majority of them will require waiting 2 years to be fully insured to the point of natural deaths!

Although you might be able to get a name-brand company however, is it really important in the event that you die due to an unnatural cause, such as a cancer or stroke? If you die in the initial 2 years under any plan, you're not covered!

Don't get one of these programs if there's no reason the money to.

Here's A secret: Work with an agent who is independent.

I am an independent last expense, whole life insurance broker. and I've done so since beginning as I believe it's important for me to compare across different insurance providers to get the best coverage for my customers like you.

A lot of agents are employed by one business. They offer only one product and offer one selection. Most of the time this isn't your best option. It's likely to cost you more and receive less coverage. In the end, you won't get you the highest value you're entitled to.

Independent agents work with a variety of firms. With each client I decide the one that will provide the most competitive price as well as that will provide the most value. My objective is to provide your 100% protection in the event of accidental or natural death within the first day of payment.

It's what I want to accomplish whenever I'm out in the field to collaborate with my clients. That's exactly what you're entitled to.

Agents who offer only items from one particular company face limitations on their underwriting. They will not be in a position to offer you the most competitive rate. In many instances the health problems you have may be a complete reason to disqualify your.

So, it's essential that you employ a last expense whole life insurance broker that is completely independent. They look at a wide range of insurers and generally have better underwriting, higher prices, and the result generally is more favorable for you.

When it comes to the final point it is your responsibility to stick by this system. For those with a fixed income you must make use of each dollar to the maximum possible extent. This is about ensuring that you're not paying more than what you are entitled to. Independent agents are more likely to achieve this.

Does Your Health Disqualify You For Final Expense Whole Life Insurance?

It's possible that you're thinking "I've already been declined." This could be an issue for anyone who is interested in a total life policy.

The good news is that health issues are generally not an issue in obtaining a job. However, it can affect your eligibility for. It's also not a factor that can completely disqualify you, even if previously you've been denied.

Some companies will offer you a lower rate regardless of having had to be rejected by other businesses. It's possible to doubt it because that's just how the firm operates.

If you've been in the industry for long enough to be an agent you know what I'm talking about. This is why you've been asked to work with multiple carriers. Why? because certain insurance companies deal with certain health concerns that other carriers don't.

It is crucial to work with an independent agent in order to obtain a better deal, more underwriting, more value and also better value for your money.

Let's discuss the most typical conditions that you could get high-quality coverage from an agent who is independent. We'll go through the list of things I'm typically seeing and offer an overview of the possibilities.

Diabetes

One of the most common is the disease known as diabetes. Many people suffer from an illness called diabetes. People are wondering what protection they are entitled to in the event of a claim.

I know a lot of patients with basic type-2 diabetes have been diagnosed at the age of adulthood. I'm able to offer them preferential insurance, even if they are insulin dependent or suffer from problems with diabetes.

In addition, I've witnessed many people suffering from diabetes neuropathy receive insurance. Most of the time, it's not a big deal. All you need to do is know the companies that work as well and which do not. Anyone with type 1 diabetes that began young in their lives can be eligible for insurance.

Lung Disease Like Copd Or Asthma

I also have a relationship with businesses that provide the an initial day of complete insurance for lung disease. Many smokers smoke for the rest of their life, just like my mother. My mom would always tell me as a child taking one of her 20th and final cigarette, "Dave, don't ever, ever start this horrible habit." The woman has stopped from then on although it's a struggle.

If you suffer from COPD or asthma or other respiratory issue it is possible that you are thinking that no insurance provider is likely to take a chance on your health. There are some companies who will provide you with a first-day complete protection for lung diseases in the majority of situations. That's a thing I'm able assist you with.

Heart Disease

If you've had a long-standing background of heart disease and you are unsure about what you are eligible for. You may have had an attack on your heart, stroke or a stent bypass seizures, aneurysms or seizures pacemaker, or some various other ailments.

We're here to inform you that, when you're with an independent agency that you trust in the event that you've had a certain amount of time from the diagnosis, you are able to be covered. I'll tell you in about a minute or so the options available to you.

Liver And Kidney Problems

A few liver or kidney problems may qualify based on the period between diagnosis and the treatment. Also, there are options for all-day coverage of neurologic issues like multiple sclerosis, lupus and Parkinson's disease.

Most people assume that in the event that they get policy, it's going to be the 2-year-wait guarantee policy. However, in the majority of situations, this isn't an actual fact.

Mental Health Issues Like Depression, Bipolar, Schizophrenia

Additionally, there are insurance companies that provide coverage for mental health conditions like bipolar disorder, depression as well as schizophrenia. Other major health concerns that could be addressed that I did not mention. I wanted to apply a an umbrella here to cover the most frequent issues.

This isn't an attempt to get the wool out of your eyes. The only choice for people is to be certain acceptance policies. They don't have any health-related concerns. In addition, you can only receive complete coverage once you have paid in for two years.

It is important to note that this is not the case in my dealings with you. I am able to get complete day coverage on the first day for a variety of circumstances. It's not a guarantee but If I'm not able to then I'll let you know this too.

Remember, it's nevertheless advisable to purchase any kind of insurance because there is a chance that you will have a longer life span than 2 years. Therefore, you shouldn't end up in a place in which you're without a plan!

Don't Wait!

If you've read so far, it's obvious that you're worried about the insurance coverage for you, your spouse or perhaps your children or parents. Do not delay!

If you've discovered a partner you can work with and be sure of, do not hesitate! A lot of people I meet have been described as "world-class procrastinators." Don't become one of them! Just just one event in your health to stop you from ever obtaining the full insurance coverage you deserve at a preferential price.

Health is on the rise now. It's a fact that age can end up creating problems, in the end, but it's easier to get better protection if you're in good health. Secure the coverage right now for a very low cost and enjoy fully covered.

One of the very first customers I wrote a policy on was a woman who had full insurance. The woman called me about a month or so after the first installment to let me know she suffered heart attacks. It is not difficult to imagine she was anxious about whether or not she'd maintain the coverage. I could assure her that she was fine. People always believe that terrible events happen to people around us however, they can happen to us as well. We have a reason why we purchase last expense insurance for whole lives.

Make Sure Your Final Expense Whole Life Insurance Stays Within Your Budget

Certain protection is better than having no coverage! Lots of parents and grandparents would like to secure huge insurance policies to leave for their children or grandchildren, however the budget may not permit the expense.

You must ensure that you're looking for a strategy that's capable of achieving your main goal. The remainder could be donated to family members. Be okay having not everything you desire, but only getting just what you need.

Be sure that the insurance policy you purchase is accessible. It's not a good thing, even for an agent to offer a policy to someone only to have them decide to cancel the policy six months further down the line. This is a waste of dollars.

I'd rather avoid buying it and then invest it in something else instead of purchasing the item and then putting it away within 6 months since you spent too much. The purchase of too much can be creating a minefield for after you're unable to afford the cost. You'll be back in the exact spot you left off with no insurance coverage.

Chapter 3: Six Steps To Buying The Best Final Expense Insurance Policy

Final expense insurance is the only insurance policy we know is needed! However, we often put it off.

If you're like the majority of my clients, then you receive a lot of junk mail as well as television ads that promote last expense life insurance.

That's the reason why I'm writing this post to help the benefit of. There's a lot of misconceptions about the last expense insurance. And, a lot of people don't know the cost-effective last expense insurance options offered to customers.

In the case of TV and junk mail companies that offer final expense insurance Most of them come with "fine print gotcha" clauses that can be a source of frustration. Indeed, the majority of people whom I speak to believe that they are not eligible for low-cost and high-quality, life insurance with a final cost.

How To Get Affordable Final Expense Life Insurance?

It is a good thing that most people be eligible for top-quality final cost insurance with great prices. The only thing you have to learn is the details, and you will be able to choose the most suitable policy.

This article was written for just this purpose! In the past year, I've observed several final expense insurance firms ripping off ordinary people. What's more shocking is that these fraudulent last expense options have name brands that which you've heard of!

The goal of this article is to provide you the necessary information to help you become more confident. When you've finished this piece, you'll know which is the most suitable final cost insurance plan. This way, family members will not have to worry about the cost of your funeral cremation or other funeral expenses.

Step 1: Final Expense Insurance Based Around Your NEEDS.

As an insurance agent for final expenses I'm here to assist people just like you to find an insurance plan that fulfills the task you'd like to achieve. If you're like many, you're in a fixed-income situation. You can only afford the maximum amount for an cost insurance policy.

When you decide to purchase an insurance policy that covers your final expenses plan, ensure you get the best plan to meet your needs!

The first requirement is you can afford it.

The first thing to do is not permit an insurance representative to persuade you to buy more insurance than you are able to afford. Instead, make sure you purchase the right plan for your budget.

There are times when you're better off the beginning of a cheaper plan. Why? because losing your last cost insurance policy can be a disaster. This is why looking for an affordable price first!

Prioritize working within your financial limits. Make sure you know your budget. Remember to consider an affordable price. Use that as your primary direction.

Step 2: What's The Best Final Expense Life Insurance - Term Or Whole?

In this article, I will explain the differences between term and full life insurance.

Term life insurance can be described as the type of insurance we refer to as "terminating insurance." Simply said, it can be cancelled at a future time. In the case of most last expense term insurance that are canceled at age 80, the date is set as the date. Since people live longer lives, a lot of people purchasing term life insurance may exceed their lifespan. Also, they will not be covered by final expense assurance... just in the time they require it!

Take a moment to think about the possibility. What would it be like in the event that you were to lose your final cost insurance? You feel like you're being scammed off, don't you think?

Term Insurance Goes Up In Price AND Cancels, Too!

That's exactly what I advise my clients. In addition, when the term life insurance plans expire and increase in cost!

If the final expense policy is crucial to you, and is something you want to have you, avoid the term life insurance. It's most likely not likely to be in your possession in the event you require it. In the event that it is the case, it's often too expensive to maintain!

How can I help? I would recommend the final expense of whole life insurance.

Life insurance that is whole never expires due to age or health and premiums are never increased and, in most cases it is completely insured and protected on the very first day. Naturally, getting complete coverage for your last expense insurance is contingent upon answering the health-related concerns. However, many people do qualify for full coverage. It is generally believed that this is the ideal type of whole life insurance policy you can have.

Let's get this straight What do you think about getting old enough to die before or even after? Don't know? Nobody does!

If you're feeling the same like you do, then the final cost whole life insurance is the best. It will be available regardless of when you die. And without ever-increasing costs that aren't affordable.

Step 3: The Truth Behind "Junk Mail" Final Expense Insurance.

Do you like watching TV? Do you receive a lot of junk mail each day? If yes, that you are exposed to all kinds of ads for the final cost insurance.

Be cautious with spam mail last cost insurance quotes! What's the reason to be cautious? The companies that provide final expense are excellent at describing their last expense insurance. Some firms are famous for calling celebrity endorsements.

Unfortunately, these last cost companies make use of celebrity endorsements and fancy-pants for a certain motive...

To DISTRACT You From The Final Expense Insurance "Fine Print!"

Are you looking for to know the "ugly" truth? A lot of the final cost life insurance providers only provide the "guaranteed acceptance" policy that provides no protection for 2 years!

In other words, if you pass away in the first two years of your life, your family members are not entitled to the entire amount!

Furthermore, many final cost insurance policies are termed as time-based insurance. In the same way that term insurance is used for the final expenses typically increase each 5 years, and then cease after 80.

What are the best way to get around this? It is necessary to work with what's known as an independent agent. Independent agents look at various final expense life insurance providers. It is the goal of an independent agent to find you the most competitive price and quality of insurance.

Additionally they offer a final expense life insurance policies that unlike anything else. People are amazed at the value they receive compared to junk mail businesses.

Choose an agent who is independent. Make sure they aren't pushing you around and is someone you be confident in, and who is interested in being a resource for you.

Step 4: Consider Working With An Independent Final Expense Insurance Broker, NOT A Captive Agent.

This is an excellent decision that everyone who's thinking about last expense insurance ought to consider taking. Let me first explain what the distinction is.

A captive last expense insurance broker is obligated to a specific life insurance company. In essence, a captive agent typically offers only one final expense choice. In most instances this option, it's neither most affordable nor does it offer the highest value when it comes to the final expense insurance!

An independent, final expense total life insurance broker gives numerous choices. If they run like you do will carry approximately 15 different insurance providers. Once they have asked clients questions about their health an independent final expense life insurance representative chooses which one is the best price for the customer. Many times, things like health and age aren't so much of an influence on the coverage.

Most of the time it can result in better prices for the customer!

The majority of people get better final cost insurance and more affordable cost. Additionally, your experience will be better. In contrast, if you are stuck with a one-trick pony final cost insurance agent it's likely to cost you more than you should and will not receive the most effective insurance coverage.

Think about this. Do you want to find the most competitive price for your last cost insurance? Would you rather cooperate with someone else who doesn't?

Many people would like the top bargain! Therefore, engaging with a professional independent total expense life insurance broker is crucial.

Step 5: How To Select The Best Final Expense Life Insurance Plan

This is a step that is related to the previous second step. It is important to have a life insurance policy that is able to meet the requirements of your family and will cover the entire cost.

In some cases, the last expense insurance policies will not fully cover the cost of the expenses that are due to be paid. Why? Since the vast majority of retirees do not have funds!

Then, what should you do if you are unable to have a plan in place which covers all the bases? Consider, "Something is better than nothing."

From my personal experience, not a single funeral home has refused to pay half the amount needed to pay for the burial of somebody. In many cases, funeral directors are willing to work together with you to find a portion of the funeral cost. It's always better to have cash than no money at all!

Step 6: How To Qualify For Final Expense Life Insurance With No Exam, And No Visit From A Salesperson.

The advancements in the qualification process for last expense life insurance allow people to obtain quality insurance without having to visit an insurance broker.

A lot of people today are not comfortable visiting a stranger. Additionally, they have become a bit sceptical about how the world works today! It's not my fault! those who do.

I've sold last expense life insurance face-to-face all my life. This is why I know that some clients have trouble with face-toface meetings.

Get Final Expense Insurance Without A Visit From An Agent!

It's the reason I've created the capability to assist individuals via phone without the need for a visit!

This is the deal. If you have to deal with someone via phone, it's important to be sure that they're genuine. This is for me to write this post to help you. I would like to share my expertise to you regarding the programs that provide final expenses for you. I'd like to prove that the possibility of getting top-quality final expense insurance with no cost of dollars. It's also done with a method that is convenient to you.

I'm now focused on helping those who aren't person-to-person in many states around the country. Chances are that if you're reading this article, I'm a licensed professional in your state, and I'm able to aid you.

If you're looking to learn how it operates, all you have to do is submit an easy application. The majority of times, this is done via telephone. There are no medical tests necessary, either. The company that will issue the final expense insurance examines your files the final expense insurance policy will usually be accepted right away. In most cases, you don't need to fill out any documentation! This is an excellent method to secure a great cheap, top-quality final cost life insurance policy without having to spend a significant amount of cash.

Next Steps To Getting Affordable Final Expense Insurance

What can you do to learn more about which options you have? As everyone's situation is unique and different states have their own firms, the most efficient option is call me at the number 888-626-0439. Or, go to buylifeinsuranceforburial.com/contact/ to send a message. We'll follow up with additional information on which options you have in terms of coverage. Be sure to fill the application entirely. This will allow us better prepare for our meeting for the most appropriate cost insurance policy that is most effectively for you.

Chapter 4: Mini Topics Related To Final Expense Insurance

No Questions Asked Life Insurance - What's The Catch?

I'm a life insurance broker working with those over 50. As a businessperson I'm frequently asked questions about the life insurance advertisements individuals receive in junk mail.

Many people are unsure of what these plans really are and typically skeptical. Actually, it is best to be skeptical about the way these life insurance plans actually function.

In reality, these insurance policies offer a two-year waiting time for deaths that are natural cause. If you are diagnosed with heart disease or cancer the insurance company will not be able to pay your death benefit in full. I have known patients who died just a few days before their two years ended, and weren't covered.

It's a shame that the variety of options available to obtain protection, even if you're fighting diabetics, COPD, cancer history the heart, cancer history and various other conditions.

Don't make the mistake of going for a no-questions-asked life insurance policy until you've looked into the other alternatives. In addition, you must speak with an independent insurance agent. He'll shop around to determine if he is able to offer you the best price. Fortunately, that's what I do at buylifeinsuranceforburial.com.

Best Burial Insurance for The Elderly

I'm going to offer you information on how to choose the most appropriate insurance plan for someone aged 60 or older. If we refer to "senior years," we're referring to someone who is typically 60 or more.

What Is Final Expense Insurance?

First thing I'm always asking my clients is "What do you want your policy to do for you?" A majority of people - I'd say that 90%would like to cover the final costs.

What are the final costs? These include funeral costs, cremation charges and any last-minute expenses they do not necessarily wish to or cannot take out from savings. An end-of-life policy may help in this way so that kids as well as beneficiaries aren't required to pay for it.

Which type of insurance policy is most suitable for seniors seeking life insurance? It's based on the kind of coverage you're looking for. The majority of people -- because they wish to be sure that the coverage will remain in place regardless of when they die seek out insurance policies that offer assurances on the price, and insurance coverage guarantees as well as a plan to be covered from the beginning of their day. In this way the majority of people do not require term insurance.

What Is Term Insurance?

Term insurance refers to the end of insurance, also known as temporary insurance. It's excellent --some of the least expensive insurance options available however the issue with term insurance is it will expire at a particular date.

In the case of, say, if you want to make sure that the loan is paid off if your death occurs unexpectedly, the term insurance is a great option. However, if you're trying to protect yourself from a funeral burial or any other expense that is final then why should you choose an insurance policy that's short-term in nature?

What Is Whole Life Final Expense?

This is why I suggest a "whole life" last expense plan, which is the ideal life insurance option for seniors. It can be as low as a few thousand dollars to $100,000. It all depends on the requirements of the customer.

The cost of insurance policies are never increased -- usually they're locked for the duration of your life. In other cases, you have to pay the insurance for a specific period of time. You then stop paying, and own the insurance just like the car you drive when you have paid off the car loan.

Additionally, coverage does not end due to medical or age. It's a great benefit that you can typically locate insurance plans that provide my customers with a first-day 100 100% coverage, regardless of whether they've had a history of illnesses. It's not a guarantee obviously. However, since I search to find the top suppliers, I am able to locate the most affordable deals for my customers.

For the summation, for first-day insurance regardless of health status it is recommended to get an all-life final cost policy.

Best Burial Insurance For People Between 86 And 90 Years Old

This post was written since the majority of companies do not offer coverage beyond 85. That means that once you reach at 86, 99 percent of employers will cut you off from receiving insurance.

These include companies like those you watch commercials on television for, and also receive spam from. But, if you're this situation, where you're years old or more and are seeking a plan to cover your last expenses, don't worry there's a plan for you to assist you in.

If you're in search of something inexpensive that covers your needs from the very first day it's possible to find a solution depending on your medical condition.

Independent Agent v. Captive Agent

I am a consultant for a variety of life insurance firms. Some of them will give you burial coverage even at the age of 86, depending on your health condition, obviously. It is just one of the advantages of using an independent agency instead of working with a captive agent.

Best Burial Insurance For People Between 50 And 60 Years Old

If it's about final cost coverage, the majority of those that we sell our products to are age 50-90. Therefore, the 50-60 year old population is somewhat distinct from older individuals in terms of health. There are also differences regarding which strategy for you and what options to steer clear of.

Better Health

The most important factor I'm able to suggest is usually with age has better health. Therefore, it's best to collaborate with someone who is a competitor and will offer you the best cost.

There are many providers that are very costly and do not make sense for those who are between the ages of 50-60. It is best to choose an agent like me working with numerous firms and look around for the most affordable price. This is the first priority.

Different Goals

The second thing to do is to be sure that the policy you choose is compatible with the purpose you are trying to reach. If your primary objective is to get just enough insurance for funeral costs, ensure you purchase what I refer to as the whole life plan. A complete life insurance policy doesn't cancel, and does not increase in cost and is securely locked with a guaranteed the first day of insurance.

The thing you should stay clear of are term insurance. The term insurance policy expires after some period of. This means that it could expire prior to you, and the cost can increase. Be aware of this and be sure to keep clear of plans if the goal is to stick with a plan throughout your life.

How To Get Life Insurance For Your Parents

If you're in your 30s or 40s, maybe older, and seeking a life insurance plan that can provide most beneficial on behalf of your grandparents, I'd encourage you to look at my web site. I'm licensed as a broker. It means I'm a broker for diverse companies. As such, I'm able to shop around and get the lowest rate and the best coverage for your needs.

Agents, I've got many years of selling to those 60 or older, who just need enough money to be buried or cremated their bodies and possibly leave some cash to their family. I've got pretty solid views on what to search for as well as what to avoid.

What To Stay Away From

The first thing to do is should stay clear of any item that arrives in the post. In general, big name businesses are usually the most expensive in this market -- AARP, Colonial Penn, MetLife, Globe. If you've seen it in the news, or even receive it by mail, it probably does not offer the greatest value.

Colonial Penn, MetLife, and Mutual of Omaha have a 2 year waiting time if someone dies due to natural reasons. In other words, if a parent experiences an accident within the initial 2 years under the policy then they will not pay for the death cost in full. They will try to hide it from you. They're quite adept at doing this. Many people don't even realize this until it's too late in the end. If you are a member of AARP or Globe and you are insured, your policy could be increased in value and end at age 80.

What To Look For

The point I want to make is they're reputable businesses however, their products can be considered to be a waste of money. The most effective thing you could get if you're in search of low-cost life insurance for parents to speak with an agent like me. As an agent for multiple businesses, my responsibility is to locate you the most affordable price as well as the highest protection.

The majority of the insurance I offer is known as total life insurance. There are other types of insurance I sell and other types, but the majority of people would like enough to put them in the ground. All life is a more affordable for a number of motives.

Never Buy Term Life Insurance For Final Expense Coverage - Here's Why

I believe that an insurance policy that covers final costs is not the best option. First, you must understand what the term "term" means. An easy way to understand the definition of insurance is to understand that the term expires. When you attain the age of a specific amount, your policy ends. When it expires, you're done with none coverage.

The first question I ask my clients who are looking for a plan to cover their funeral is do you desire plans that will allow you to be unable to live? More precisely are you aware of what time you'll pass away? Naturally, everyone says, "No, I don't know when I am going to die, and I don't want to outlive my coverage." If this is your answer you're probably saying that you shouldn't be looking at an insurance policy for term purposes.

What Else Is There?

Why would anyone think about the possibility of them? Since they're extremely affordable compared to whole life insurance. The term "whole life" is not the same as the term. It doesn't end due to age.

prices never rise and coverage, when you have an independent agent, like my own, will begin from the day you first start. There are times when we only protect you. However, most of the time it is possible to be completely protected. This isn't a guarantee although we're able to provide it.

It's important to note that our demise is uncertain. I'm not sure the date I'll pass away. I'm 31. My life could end sooner than you will, regardless of whether you're in your 50's 60's or in your 70's. What's important to remember is that we must have a plan to ensure that we never die and that is at hand no matter when the moment is.

Chapter 5: Best Burial Insurance For Memory Disorders

In reality, it's almost impossible to obtain something that doesn't have a memory condition. The majority of memory-related conditions are categorized into dementia or Alzheimer's. In this case, you'll may lose some memory capacity, both in the short and long term. capacity for memory.

It is true that there is no other option in life insurance that a guaranteed issue insurance plan. The way to think about it is this. The majority of companies will not talk to you about taking Aricept or Namenda or another cognition-related memory medication.

But, it is possible to buy a plan. However, anyone with any of them plans will only have protection for a period of two years.

If you die due to natural causes, the beneficiary will receive interest in addition to the cash paid into. If you are beyond the waiting time and the policy is paid out fully.

That means that you must be older than two years before the full coverage comes into in.

This is so that there are options. If you've tried to contact someone before but were rejected, contact them. It's easy. I've got carriers who can offer you protection for these problems. I do my research to determine the most affordable burial insurance rates. This way, you gain from paying the lowest amount that is possible.

Chapter 6: Best Burial Insurance For Cancer History

Let me provide an overview of what I mean by cancer, and give you the options you have. The first thing to consider is whether you meet the criteria depends on whether or not you're currently diagnosed with cancer, or whether there's been a long time since you've had cancer. There are different options available to each stage and I'll go into more detail on what the choices are.

What is the exact meaning of what I am referring to when I refer to cancer? If I use the word "cancer," it's really the usual kind of cancer that you're thinking of. It can spread across the body, and then infect various parts of the body. In the case of, say, if you have basal cell skin cancer, it's not the type of cancer that we're discussing. It is possible to get total coverage at a discounted price for this type of cancer.

In the event that you suffer from what is usually thought of as cancer like lung cancer, prostate cancer, etc The type of insurance that you are eligible for depends on the time. What is the duration of your cancer? When did you stop treatment? Was your last time you had treatment? Let's take a look.

You Have Cancer Currently.

If you're currently diagnosed with cancer, the most effective option is to get a guarantee issue plan. A guaranteed issue allows you to be approved for the plan but does not completely cover naturally-caused cause. In other words, if you suffer from cancer during the first 2 years of all guaranteed issue policies, they'll only pay back the cost that you put into the plan, and a tiny amount of interest. However, the flipside is that if you survive beyond two years, the policy will cover the complete amount. Absolutely no questions asked, regardless of whether you were diagnosed with cancer at the time that you bought the policy. The benefit of this policy is that you're covered completely from the very first day to cover accidental causes of death in accordance with the policy.

Cancer-Free For A Year Or More

In the next instance, suppose that you've had cancer-free status for more than one year. After that you might be eligible for a life insurance graded policy. The way to describe the term "graded" life insurance" means that you are covered in part starting the first day. In other words, if you die in the following day, or so after the date of effectiveness and they give you a percentage of the face value in the plan.

It is generally between 30 and 45percent. If you purchased an insurance policy worth $10,000 that would result in a payment of between $3000 and $4500, depending upon how the policy appears and the level the policy is defined as through. An average payout of 30% is much more than none. The majority of companies require you to be patient for two, three and even four years before they speak to you about having suffered from cancer. It's a great way to be to be recorded when you've been cancer free for a longer period of time.

Cancer-Free For 2+ Years

Are you looking at the next two or three years after treatments and cancer? There's plenty of options that offer you the an initial day of complete coverage. It is important to make use of this as fast as you can. It's not difficult to obtain. All you have to do is talk with someone like me who is a broker for various firms and is able to make you eligible for plans.

Chapter 7: Best Burial Insurance For Depression, Bipolar, And Schizophrenia

In the first place, when I refer to a mental health concern is a mental health issue, I mean things as simple as bipolar or depression, or something more serious and treated like schizophrenia. Three of them are the most common mental health problems I'm speaking about. Most people have heard that it's possible to operate with difficulties when you're well treated. It's good to know that the majority of these businesses acknowledge the importance of this.

Depression

In the case of depression, it's simple to receive your first day insurance, regardless of the kind of depression. It's okay. It's a breeze to acquire it, and I have to deal with daily.

Bipolar

Bipolar is a little more challenging than other disorders, but I've access to businesses that are glad to work together. There are clients who were treated with medications similar to lithium in treating bipolar disorder. You can obtain protection. This isn't a matter of concern for us at all.

Schizophrenia

The third issue is schizophrenia. Schizophrenia, which I'm pleased to say, is easy to qualify for, no matter if you've suffered from it for the rest of your existence. There are many people who can remain on medications with no problems, and we're able to get insurance coverage that many doctors can't.

Chapter 8: Best Burial Insurance For Cardiac Issues

People believe that medical issues will void burial insurance benefits. This isn't an accurate assumption! As long as you've been in good health between the last health check will give you many opportunities to buy high-quality life insurance to cover your final costs. Let's take a look at it in detail.

Heart Attack, Stroke, Stents, Bypass, Aneurysms, Pacemaker History Within The Past 12 Months

If you've experienced the occurrence of a stroke, heart attack as well as a stent implant or open-heart bypass, aneurysm or pacemaker implanted in the last twelve months, a guaranteed issue final expense policy is the ideal life insurance plan.

What Is Guaranteed Issue Life Insurance?

Life insurance with guaranteed issue is intended to provide coverage regardless of health status. In the event that you suffer a death due to unnatural causes Guaranteed issue life insurance will limit the death benefit in the initial two years.

Also, although you're insured to the fullest extent for accidental deaths however, any cause that is natural for death that is due to heart disease or otherwise - does not guarantee the beneficiaries of your estate a complete death benefit payment.

Why Would I Want To Get A Plan Like That?

In the event that a guaranteed-issue life insurance plan is the only one my clients can get They often ask "Why even bother with a burial insurance plan that doesn't cover from the first day?" This is my reasons for getting a guaranteed issue cost insurance plan. While it's not fully coverage for natural death on the first day.

Your Health Could Change At Any Moment

Let's face it. There is a chance that you will suffer another heart attack or health issues.

There is a chance that you will develop a new type of disease, like diabetes. Or your doctor may prescribe you a new medication.

What's the reason? because ALL possible health issues in the future could hinder your eligibility to receive a quality life insurance policy to cover final costs. If you do not wait until there are more suitable options in burial insurance, adverse changes to your health can render you ineligible for better options.

This means you might be waiting 2 years before the normal death coverage kicks in... at which point you should have been insured. If you got the final cost coverage earlier!

Hope this helps!

I am fortunate that a majority of my patients suffering from heart disease are aware of this. They also purchase plans that guarantee issue. Why? My customers know that the delay in getting insured is risky.

Heart Attack, Stroke, Stents, Bypass, Aneurysms, Pacemaker History Within The Past 1 To 2 Years

Did you experience any heart-related medical event within the last 12-24 months? If yes, then you could be eligible for some great final expense options.

You could, for example, be eligible for a "standard," first-day, 100% coverage as well as the "graded" plan, which is partially covered beginning on the date of buying the burial insurance policy. Some agents do not offer such options. But, last expense insurance agents like me offer them!

Call or email me in the event that you are in the criteria for this. I'm here to assist you.

Heart Attack, Stroke, Stents, Bypass, Aneurysms, Pacemaker History - 2 Years Or Greater Since The Event Took Place

If your having a heart attack or circulatory issue that happened more than two years ago and you're eligible for full first-day, initial cost protection. Actually, most firms that offer final expense coverage will take your case at a discounted rate!

There are however a number of aspects to take into consideration before you decide on the best price qualification.

Do you, for instance, consume blood thinners, like Coumadin, Warfarin, or Plavix?

Do you also use isosorbide or Nitroglycerin? Although some burial insurance providers take these medications, many don't.

It is recommended to work with an expert in final expenses like me. Brokers are able to navigate the choices for you to find the most suitable option for you, based on your particular circumstance.

What Cardiac And Heart Health Issues Are ALWAYS Considered Guaranteed-Issue Life Insurance?

Sadly, certain conditions of the heart do not get first-day complete coverage. We'll discuss those issues below.

Congestive Heart Failure And Burial Insurance

The condition of congestive heart failure can cause it to cause water accumulation within the heart. This is a serious heart problem that doesn't completely go out of the body. It's unfortunate that the majority of last-cost carriers provide only the option of a guarantee-issue.

But, one last expense company could be able to provide you with "graded," partial first-day coverage. Although it is possible however, I've seen very that very few people qualify for coverage since there are other health issues that hinder the applicants from being eligible.

Angina, Nitroglycerin Usage For Final Expense Insurance

If you're prescribed isosorbide mononitrate or nitroglycerin or are suffering from angina it is more difficult getting a fully-covered final expense insurance.

For burial insurance companies Nitrate medicines are an automatic denial. The carriers will provide a waiting period and a guaranteed-issue choice. However, this doesn't happen with every carrier. But, I do prepare my clients for this.

Angina is part of the same situation, in that Nitrates can treat angina.

Other Cardiac And Circulatory Diseases

Let's take a take a look at some other circulatory conditions that could qualify for life insurance.

Seizure History

Certain insurance companies deny coverage to people with who have a history of seizures or prescribe medications to avoid seizures. But, some insurance companies whom I deal with are accepting in the case of seizures as well as seizure preventative medication.

Examples of this are medications like Keppra or Dilantin are accepted by a lot of companies for first-day coverage and with a discount! Also, some selected companies allow applicants with a experience of seizures, and.

In all cases it is all about the overall health of the candidate. However, it is important to understand this. You can get someone who has had recent seizures or one who is taking seizure prevention medication, to get the first day of all-inclusive coverage.

If you contact me, I'll figure out what I can help you.

Pacemakers And Life Insurance

Many insurance providers consider pacemaker implants as a cardiac operation, which is comparable to strokes or heart attacks in previous history. Some insurance companies will offer first-day protection for patients with pacemakers who are older than 12 months from the date of installation.

Are you experiencing an upgrade to the battery on your pacemaker? If yes, then you could have the opportunity to get preferred day-one coverage since some companies don't consider change in the battery as cardiac event.

Diabetes With Heart Disease History

Some insurers are hesitant to accept those who have a diagnosis of diabetes when combined with a cardiovascular or heart medical history. Why? Research has shown that diabetes can exacerbate and increase the possibility of having problems with your heart. Thus, the underwriters for insurance carriers for certain carriers may raise the amount of the coverage you receive at your last expense.

This is the great news. I research the top last expense companies to find which one offers the most suitable burial insurance. In many cases I come across alternatives that aren't concerned about a mix of the history of your heart and diabetes.

Chapter 9: Best Burial Insurance For Diabetes

Since I was authorized to market final expense insurance back in 2011 I've had the pleasure of meeting a lot of people who feel that having a diagnosis of diabetes restricts possibilities for coverage under life insurance.

It's a good thing I've got some great new! With the correct final expense insurance provider You'll be able to choose from a wide range of top-quality last expense options, regardless of the fact that you have diabetes. In the end, it's important to partner with an agent. They can help you find for the most affordable and top quality companies that are available.

Diagnosed With Diabetes And Only Taking Pills Or Managed With Diet

Many people suffering from diabetes take only medications. In addition, a lot of people with an diagnosis of diabetes and are able to manage their food consumption have the ability to control their diabetes and without medication.

This is the great positive news. If you're the only type of diabetes you suffer from the options for cost coverage are brilliant! The good news is that most insurance providers can be flexible when it comes to a simple diabetes diagnosis.

As a summary, you can rest confident that you'll be able to qualify to receive high-quality coverage of final expenses provided that you have diabetes is managed through diet or pills.

Diabetes Managed With Insulin

Then things become somewhat complicated. There are many insurance companies that will provide coverage to those who suffer from insulin. But, there are some factors to consider first in order to identify an appropriate company to collaborate with.

Did You Start Insulin After The Age Of 50?

If you began taking insulin treatment after the age of 50, you are eligible to receive the majority of final expense insurance choices. In simple terms, the aim is to locate the business that offers the most competitive price and quality.

Did You Start Insulin In Your 40s?

In your 40s, the time to start insulin is earlier than when most people who are diabetic begin with insulin. It's good to know that we can offer you a quality last expense insurance at no cost when you first started taking insulin in the 40s.

Are You A Type 1 Diabetic?

Typ 1 diabetics can be described as people who suffer from diabetes who are diagnosed as children. In general, Type 1 diabetics use insulin prior to the age of 10 or a little later. The past has been that Type 1 Diabetics have had problems obtaining adequate coverage. But, now it's possible to obtain final cost insurance even with having a Typ one Diabetic diagnosis.

In the end, it's important to partner with an agent who can help you shop for the top carriers. We can do that.

Complications Of Diabetes

People who suffer from complications with diabetes are often difficult to cover. There are a variety of circumstances to take into consideration.

Diabetic Neuropathy

In the event that a diabetic is beginning to experience pain in their legs, feet, or hands, it is likely that it is due to diabetic neuropathy.

In reality, lots of are unable to qualify for the full insurance coverage if they have a diabetic neuropathy diagnosis. But, we are able to connect with carriers who accept diabetic patients that offer high-quality final expense insurance. Call us today for further information.

Nephropathy And Amputations Due To Diabetes

They are also more difficult to treat. Nephropathy is first and foremost an consequence of diabetes since it can affect kidneys. As well, amputations can be caused by uncontrolled diabetes.

We're still able to aid you. We'll have to ask specific questions in order to understand the options available to you.

Chapter 10: Best Burial Insurance For Kidney Issues

Kidney issues are an extremely difficult subject to address within the life insurance market. However, it's possible to obtain decent coverage for an affordable price, if you are in a certain situation. This is why I'm going list some of the different circumstances that can be classified as kidney-related issues, and look into the options.

The most frequent kidney issue we come across is end-stage renal impairment that requires dialysis. The kidneys can't perform on their own, and require assistance from dialysis services three times every week. In the clinic, doctors cleanse and treat your blood in order to ensure you stay well. Actually, if you don't have it your blood, you'll surely die.

End-stage renal diseases are an incurable condition which is why there aren't any insurance companies who can provide coverage for the first day. The only choice available is an insurance policy with a waiting period of two years. It means you'll have to be patient for two years following the time you have taken out the insurance before being completely insured.

If you pass away through accident, you will receive 100% coverage beginning the moment that you purchased the policy. Be aware that in the case of the natural causes of death, like kidney diseases, there are none. There is always a wait of two years. I've been in the business for quite a long time I've spoken with a lot of dialysis patients, as well as insurance firms. There is no alternative other than this.

The end-stage kidney disease without dialysis is the point where things can get very exciting. There are several stages prior to dialysis. This is why the term "end-stage" comes into play due to the fact that there are several stages between. If you suffer from kidney issues like kidney function declines, yet your body performs, there are choices to help. There are several insurance companies which will provide you with complete coverage there is no graded coverage under certain conditions if you're suffering from kidney problems, but not total and complete inability.

It's based on a number of variables, including prescription medication and medical history. However, it's extremely difficult to find a reliable insurance provider specifically for this matter. If you suffer from end-stage renal disease is the case, then you're considering the possibility of dialysis in the near future. You should secure a plan that will cover you starting the day you sign up.

The other scenario is in the event that you've received an organ transplant. If you've ever experienced an organ transplant, irrespective of whether it's a kidney, or not, your sole choice is waiting for two years. That's the only way to go however. The anti-rejection medication you're taking for all the time. In reality, an organ transplant isn't certain to happen. If you find yourself in the same situation, know that the most effective thing you can take is to secure an affordable price for an effective two-year waiting time such as a Gerber's item.

BEST BURIAL INSURANCE FOR RESPIRATORY ISSUES

The chronic lung condition is one of the most difficult concerns to deal with when it comes to the final funeral insurance.

Chronic Respiratory Disease

Many companies operating that deal in burial insurance combine all chronic diseases. Examples include chronic obstructive pulmonary disorder or emphysema and tuberculosis and chronic bronchitis are thought to be of the same degree. It is the case for all conditions that require continuous treatment by inhalers, such as Spiriva and Advair. Proair or the use of oxygen.

COPD

In the meantime, as medicines improve and more businesses are now allowing patients with COPD to have full day coverage for certain circumstances. There are a number of companies offering smoking smokers with 100% coverage and COPD sufferers, which is great!

The one possible exception is when there are numerous issues connection with COPD. As an example, extremely bad chronic heart issues or even more serious situations of COPD that require continuous oxygen consumption may make it harder. The use of oxygen is an ongoing issue that doesn't go away. So, there are limited companies who offer full coverage on the first day to those who are using oxygen.

But that doesn't mean you won't be able to obtain coverage. However, it's is a lot more challenging. If you're taking oxygen, the best option is to purchase a waiting time of two years product. That means that you must wait for two years until the coverage of natural deaths kicks into effect. It is covered 100% for death due to accident, but there is no coverage for natural causes.

What Can You Do?

This is to inform you that you're limited to options if you're in need of oxygen. However, we are able to get protection that's reasonable if have an independent agent like me in order to research and negotiate you the most competitive price.

Rarely, there are instances when a person has COPD however, they don't require any kind of continuous treatment. So, they don't have any history of medical prescriptions filled during the last several years.

If you are in this group you are likely to obtain coverage on your first day at a discounted rate. Although this is an one exception it is possible to enhance coverage for individuals who are typically restricted to higher cost plans or even a waiting period of two years.

Chapter 11: Best Burial Insurance For Hiv
AND AIDS PATIENTS

In the past year, I've met many people suffering from AIDS or HIV diagnosis. The life insurance industry has historically aren't able to accept final expense insurance to people with such ailments.

It's a good thing! Even with HIV and AIDS diagnosis, it's now more accessible than ever before to be eligible for life insurance coverage that is affordable which is specifically designed to take care of the final costs and to replace the income.

Options For Final Expense Coverage With An HIV Positive Diagnosis

Late in 2015, many companies launched new last expenses life insurance plans to HIV positive people. In particular, these firms offered insurance to top-quality HIV positive people for top-quality life insurance.

In the present, if you're HIV positive and you age falls between 30-60, you might be eligible to purchase a 10 or 15-year insurance term through a major life insurance provider.

You'll also find additional information about how you can qualify for the 10 or 15-year term life insurance policies:

The maximum life insurance coverage is $2,500,000.00

The applicant must be an U.S. Resident.

The guidelines for medical underwriting can be described as follows:

* HIV is not a result of the use of intravenous drugs.

* It is not possible to have Hepatitis B and Hepatitis C.

* No Tuberculosis. the nontuberculous abacterial disease

* HIV diagnosis longer than 12 months.

*6 months or more from the time you began the antiretroviral treatment.

* Current count of CD4 less than 350 and performed in the past 6 months

* The lowest CD4 count is greater 200. There is no previous history of having an AIDS diagnosis.

Final Expense Life Insurance For AIDS Diagnosis

Some of you reading this might be suffering from already received an AIDS diagnosis and are wondering which programs they can qualify to be eligible for. Although AIDS patients are now eligible for coverage of final expenses however, these programs are different from those available for HIV positive patients. Check out the following article to learn more.

No Questions Asked Life Insurance For AIDS Patients

At the time of writing this article No-questions-asked life insurance is the only option to those who have been diagnosed with AIDS.

The life insurance policy that is no-questions-asked is pretty self-explanatory. The policy is purchased by the applicant without asking any health related inquiries. This includes questions regarding AIDS.

Pros And Cons Of No-Questions Asked Life Insurance

The benefits of the no-questions-asked life insurance plan:

* You do not need to undergo a medical examination

* You don't need to answer any health-related questions.

The coverage cannot be denied provided you meet the criteria for age.

In essence, if you are able to make your name known, then you're certified!

There are a few disadvantages of life insurance with no questions asked to cover final costs:

* Natural causes of death is limited to the first 2 years.

In the end, should you die from circumstances, your beneficiary will receive a refund of your premiums, along with ten percent interest (some greater, others lesser).

Remember that this covers all natural causes for death. Although I prefer securing my clients in the event of natural death, I do not want my clients suffering from having an AIDS diagnosis are left with that option as the sole one.

Think Long-Term

The reason why you purchase final cost life insurance, if you're not covered right away?

The first step is to start coverage earlier. This allows you to reach complete coverage sooner. Think about putting off the purchase of the final expense insurance policy due to the fact that you're frustrated because not being able to get the complete coverage.

No matter how much you hate it however, you'll need to wait at least two years to receive natural death protection. You're delaying the inevitable. Your family is in danger! My clients have died after two years of waiting. If they had not had insurance the family could have been in financial trouble paying for funeral expenses and the cost of their final expense.

I'm thankful for recent developments in insurance options for AIDS as well as HIV patients. You can, thankfully, find quality, high-quality final expense life insurance with much less hassle than ever before.

BEST BURIAL INSURANCE FOR NEUROLOGICAL DISORDERS

For starters, I describe neurological conditions as those that include Parkinson's, sclerosis Lou Gehrig's Disease, as well as other conditions that impact your nervous system. Most people suffer from problems like these for a long time. There's no cure. Sometimes, they're easily treated. However, there are times when they're unmanageable.

Parkinson's

For instance, Parkinson's disease is treatable and the majority of insurance providers recognize the fact that. So, they're either offering you complete or partial protection. I strive to give my customers full coverage on their first day.

If you suffer from Parkinson's disease I would like to hear from you. I'll be able to provide you with several options in life insurance policies that a majority of representatives can.

Lou Gehrig's

If you are suffering from Lou Gehrig's disease, then you could be eligible for day coverage. Conditions like lupus and multiple Sclerosis can be long-lasting, however they can be controlled.

I'm here to assist you in getting all-encompassing coverage from the beginning of the day to either one of these issues. This is possible. All you have to do is work with someone who will shop around to find the most affordable price. The majority of these businesses appear on television aren't going to provide you with the most competitive bargain.

Chapter 12: Best Burial Insurance For Smokers

Since I received my life insurance certificate since 2011, I've come across many tobacco smokers. A lot of these users are concerned about the cost they'll pay for funeral insurance.

Although smoking tobacco can increase the cost of insurance, working with the appropriate agent will reduce the amount you pay for burial insurance. You don't want to spend over what is necessary, do you?

Tobacco Users - Avoid These Burial Insurance Products!

The first thing to do is. Be sure that when you request quotes on burial insurance to do not opt for "guaranteed acceptance life insurance," or "no-questions asked life insurance."

While the prices may appear to be competitive, these plans don't offer one day coverage. What exactly does this mean? If you die during the initial two years of your policy, the beneficiary of the policy does not receive the complete death benefits.

The beneficiary actually is paid the amount of premiums repaid together with interest. That's horrible!

Consider it this way. If you pass away due to natural causes 12 months after the start of the guaranteed acceptance of your life insurance policy, your beneficiary could only get a few hundreds of dollars in compensation. This isn't enough to pay for the funeral.

What are you supposed to do? It is important to ensure that you are working with an agent. Brokers look through a range of inexpensive burial insurance firms. This means you have more chance of finding premium, high-quality burial insurance with full coverage and all for a reasonable cost.

What If I Smoke And Have COPD?

Smokers may have the COPD diagnosis. In addition, they may be concerned that the diagnosis will make them ineligible to get quality insurance.

The good news is that. when working with brokers, you'll generally find full coverage on the first day. Even if you've got an diagnosis of COPD as well as emphysema and lung diseases.

Many companies that appear on television and on the internet force the customer to wait for 2 years before securing your family against deaths due to natural causes. You can increase your chance of being protected from this, and get an agent.

What If I Smoke Cigars?

In the past, smokers of cigars tend to have a better chance of being eligible for insurance on life as compared to smokers. However, this may not be the case all the time however, smokers of cigars may qualify for preferential rates that are not tobacco-related generally speaking.

In the Buy Life Insurance for Burial We partner with insurance companies that evaluate smoking cigars at rates that are not tobacco-related. In a variety of situations, we have saved our clients hundreds of dollars each year for their insurance for life. How? We work with companies who consider smokers of cigarettes as having less severe negative health effects, as compared to smokers of cigarettes.

The frequency of smoking does not matter. In addition, a smoking of cigars is permitted daily while still qualifying to receive non-smoker rate.

What If I Dip Or Chew Tobacco?

It could be because I'm in the Southeast However, I frequently meet people who use cigarettes or use dip snuff. Many are concerned that they can't pay the higher prices related to tobacco use.

Thankfully, insurance companies consider smoking and chewing like smoking cigars. They are both considered to be non-smokers rate by several insurance companies.

How To Secure The Best Rates For Tobacco Users

Make sure that you're working with an agent. This will give you the best certainty that you'll receive the highest value for your burial insurance as a user of tobacco.

In addition, the price of burial insurance for smokers vary widely. There are price differences for burial insurance that range from 40 to $50 per month. These are all for the same insurance plans.

Chapter 13: What Is The History Of Insurance?

The concept of insurance was first introduced far back in the 3rd and 2nd millennium BC. Chinese, Babylonian and Indian traders used the concept of insurance to transfer and distribute the risks involved in their business actions. Charles Duhigg says that since the 17th century, the insurance industry have become the leading experts in risk. In particular, between 1750-1755, between 1750 and 1755, the Codex Hammurabi Law formulated a law that required that any sea captain, captain, or charterer who could save a vessel from total loss not required to make payments of 50% of the value of the vessel to the owner of the vessel.

Our forefathers' practice was a great way to save money. But, as time has passed we've seen improvements in the quality of insurance system, inclusiveness of insurance policies as well as a rising number of insurance companies. Insurance is always changing. The risks our forefathers feared against loss resolved over time, opening the way for an entirely new risk. Like, for instance, risks in the business sector which were uninsurable prior to the Covid-19 epidemic have now become insurable after the Covid-19 pandemic.

The consequences of insurable climate change depend on current social, environmental, and technological environment. Political shifts can create more risky insurable ones. In particular fighting between Russian and Ukraine conflict has created potential dangers to businesses arising from violent political conflict. War can bring about negative consequences on business. Take a look at the wars in the world and the way that business was hit hard.

Current Insurance Trends

The risks of technology have been increasing as a result of the war between Russia and Ukraine. In light of the news regarding the conflict, Russia has resorted to cyber-attacks to retaliate against Ukraine as well as NATO states. A rise in cyberattacks poses an extremely high-risk digital threat which could leave people grieving or even dying. Because of the digitization of the personal and government goods and services the world has increased vulnerability to cyberattacks as well as security failures. As a result, companies could be impacted by high overheads due to faulty operational system.

As a result of the climate shift and the actions taken, much has been changed. Today, we face new risks linked to climate change. This includes the destruction of infrastructure in the coastal areas as a result of the rise in sea level. A prime example is the aftermath of Hurricane Sandy which struck New York City.

In the wake of changes in climate the agricultural output has drastically decreased in certain regions of the United States. A report from the national government on impacts on the economy from climate change in the United States has shown that the Midwestern and Southern counties are likely to experience greater than 10% decline in agriculture over the next 20 years.

What Does Insurance Offer?

Insurance provides a safety net for the risk of occurrence. Have you experienced the numerous advantages of taking Insurance. It is possible to gain great extent by taking insurance. First of all, insurance for health is at the forefront of safeguarding young people against imminent financial crisis. Medicaid has provided assistance to thousands of homeless children and disabled youngsters. Medicaid has also extended its services for children and teens who are leaving foster care.

Children in foster care are at risk of health problems due to mental health issues such as disability, drug use and mental illness. Health insurance has been an important lifesaver for many youngsters. Yet, a large portion of young people don't have insurance. Based on data from the Urban Institute, 49% of youth are covered by employer-sponsored insurance, while 10% are covered by Medicaid or another public insurance as well as another 10% are covered by non-group health coverage. This translates into about 31% of young people uninsured. This may seem like it's a tiny number but that the effect is massive as we all be a part of the impact.

Second, property insurance can help many people empower them and their families through having their own businesses as well as properties like land, structures as well as machinery. Similar to how Millard Drexler said that it is impossible to run a business without risking and succeeding in pursuing our dreams by following our dreams regardless of the cost. Through this type of insurance will ensure that you receive a steady stream of revenue from your business, while making substantial investments, and acquiring assets. This is the way you can plan your future.

Why Buy Insurance?

Being without life, property, or health insurance can be very risky. It is a gamble with your finances, life as well as your health, property and life. Make the decision to become more of a planner, be a responsible gambler.' In working with an insurance firm has been a positive experience for some but others not so good. In the present, focus on instances where people have appreciated the work of insurance companies in providing a boost to their customers and rescuing them from a huge financial burdens. In the case of are automobile accidents, business losses or outbreaks of disease, Insurance has chipped in and helped make the circumstances less stressful. Insurance can transform you in such a way that you forget that once you were an abyss. It's why it's so important to invest in Insurance.

Companies that provide insurance ensure their reliability by using Reinsurance, which is a method to decrease risk. Reinsurance is an insurance policy that companies purchase to protect their business from the disproportionate loss that results due to a large amount of exposure. Reinsurance is a crucial part of the efforts of insurance companies to safeguard their financial security.

In the case of studies that suggest a very low chance that a storm will affect any particular area the insurance firm could offer a large amount in hurricane-related insurance. If something unimaginable happened and a hurricane struck in the area, then the company could suffer massive losses. The insurance companies could go out of business whenever an natural catastrophe strikes, in the event that reinsurance does not eliminate some risk out of the equation.

However, certain people find it difficult to acquire Insurance. One of the main reasons are the lack of employment and an incorrect notion of insurance. The increasing digitalization of goods and services, there are many people who are not employed. Covid-19 has led to an increase in unemployment as more people were laid-off and reprenched. The absence of employment prevents you from obtaining insurance coverage provided by your employer and increases the amount you earn for insurance costs.

It is possible to play an important contribution to improving your quality of life with insurance. Your own personal barriers to health, growth and security financially. It is important to recognize the ways in which we can cause our own misery. Similar to how Manoj Arora states that life insurance can be a mitigation from the risks of existence, financial freedom can be described as an assurance to having a good life! Your choice has always been yours. This day, I am challenging you to think about your lifestyle as well as your health and assets. Imagine losing any or more of these assets because of lack of knowledge. It is not wise to listen to the insights we gave during the numerous discussions, only to dismiss them. Implementing this information will be beneficial and affect our generation as well as the generations before us.

Insurance Feeds Lifestyle

It is possible that insurance will become our way of life If we keep it as a way of life. When we practice, it becomes easier to achieve. It is possible that we are not in the position we'd like to be right now however, we have the ability to make a decision to become what we'll have in the next. Take the initiative. Be a responsible individual and work hard to ensure your financial security. It is possible to start investing into Insurance by using what you've got. Dwayne "The Rock," Johnson stated that the success of all things will come down on focus and determination which you can control.

Securing financial freedom and security by utilizing insurance. Earn returns on your payments for premiums to insurance companies. This is the only way towards financial independence that many suffer from due to lack of decision-making skills, ignorance and lack of discipline. Are you not looking for financial freedom? The money you earn is the goal for Insurance.

Learn to improve your knowledge. There's no limit to how much you know. Make sure you are studying Insurance. It is essential to know the basics before making decisions about risk. It is important to know what you're signing up to in advance. So, you create an approach to protect your self from the risks. Making a conscious effort to improve your self-esteem gives you the desire to continue learning. The process of learning can transform you which is a key factor in your development across all facets of your life.

Based on this information, you have been given the task of attracting people to join to secure your future. You can be a great ambassador of Insurance. Increase awareness of life, health and home insurance. This way you can positively influence the lives of others, which can be your strength.

Insurance is an essential part of every person's life. As you venture into the world, and as you are pursuing your career or your dream job it is important to not allow fear of losing to prevent the growth you're pursuing.

It won't completely eliminate losses, however it reduces your risk as an individual, and ultimately help you save money.

Life Insurance

There's nothing more vital than your life as well as your capacity to earn a living. Therefore, it makes sense to protect your most valuable assets - yourself! This is an excellent idea that I am in agreement in that safeguarding the future of your family is your duty.

Chapter 14: What Is Life Insurance?

The life insurance policy has diversified throughout time, to accommodate our various needs. Insurance policies that protect you allow the insurer to compensate the insured for event of calamity. It could be the death of a terminal illness or disability. One of the most recent policies implemented in the life insurance sector is called term insurance.

The majority of us had thought about this possibility. The time frame for insurance is very short and can be as short as 10, 20 and 30 years. There are a variety of options available particularly after the period has ended. It is possible to reduce the duration of insurance, change it into permanent life insurance, or bake it. There are many options available and all are designed to fit the diverse needs of our financial situation.

However the investment policy is an option to save. The policy allows you to make capital payments through annual or lump sum premiums. At the time of expiration, the period of insurance, you can earn the interest earned along with the principal. The federal government offers the tax deferral option for life insurance policies that is an excellent bargain. We all know about all-life insurance as well as universal life and diverse universal life insurance in this class.

Based on the individual's preferences There is a lot of flexibility in selecting between life insurance that is whole and the term insurance. Whole life insurance, is one of the options that ensures coverage for life in cash value as well as non-stop costs. Term insurance is useful for resolving short-term financial issues and offers a variety of up thirty years.

Universal Health insurance is a type of life insurance which will pay for costs for hospitalization, such as medical consultations with a doctor and. It is the World Health Organization has partnered with the US government in providing all-inclusive health insurance to the citizens of America. A good example is the daily health deducts via medical insurance ID cards. The value of the card has increased from at an average of $2405 from 2021, and then to around $2825 in 2022.

When to Buy Life Insurance?

Health history, age as well as gender are the main factors in the life insurance policy. Latest data regarding rates of insurance show that the rates for people who are 70 years old is 1000% higher than rates for a 30 year old. What can that mean? Age plays a significant role in the determination of prices. If you can pay earlier for life insurance, the higher. When you are in your 20s, you have lower costs that those older than 60. Also, gender plays a role in prices. Incredibly, girls and women are more likely to live longer as compared to males.

In the case of premiums, a variance isn't the only thing that happens. There are different bonus amounts based on the type of type of life insurance you select. Term life insurance generally offers lower rates than total life insurance. This is because of the differences in time when the cash accumulates. It has been established the beneficiaries are reimbursed for the insured's demise.

The investment in a life insurance firm can help make sure that the family of the deceased will be financially stable following the passing. It's a bit depressing to be grieving and experience financial stress at the same time, isn't that be? You can avoid all of these by preparing ahead. In particular, families with young children are advised to get life insurance as minors will be lost upon the demise of both or one parent. A different group of individuals who require insurance for life are those who co-own the home, parents who have adults who have special needs or funeral benefits.

The additional benefit that comes with an insurance policy for life that is not subject to the cost of interest and. This payout is completely uncomplicated. Funeral arrangements are covered within this package too. Beneficiaries also get gains on savings, specifically in the case of the whole life insurance. They are freed from having to constantly struggle to cover living costs after the loss of a dear person. The benefits of this are accessible to all of us.

There are five insurance firms you could work with in order to reap these benefits.

* Haven Life insurance company is one of the top service providers in the category of life insurance. Its services are accessible on their web site. It is easy to purchase and maintain the life insurance policy from the privacy of your own living room. These sophisticated technology methods have greatly aided the success of this firm. The customers they serve receive premium protection limits that can reach three million dollars from 5 to 30 years old. The access to digital wills and fitness apps is a

given. The apps don't require medical tests this is an advantage for those who appreciate the convenience. But, on the flip side the application is restricted only to individuals aged 64 and under. It also doesn't have the option of a permanent insurance plan.

* Bestow Life insurance company offers low-cost life insurance to individuals who are between the ages of 18 to 60. The coverage limits vary from $50,000 up to $1,500,000. Applications are easy to fill out, and you receive an instant quote as well as acceptance to join the business. Alongside this is the 30-day trial period to test the policy before you agree to the policies guidelines.

* New York Life Insurance renders diverse services including general, term and whole-life insurance policies that provide cash value and earn an interest rate on the money you invest. These policies are quite expensive, and come with unclear

protection limits and rules. As an example, a woman who is 35 years old costs $142.67 per month for a one million insurance plan over 20 years.

* North Western Mutual Life Insurance Company provides the entire range of life insurance choices swiftly and easily. The insurance is not accessible online which is why one needs to get in touch with an agent to request an estimate. They cover more than 1 million.

* Mass Mutual Life insurance offers security in the financial market and an improved pay-off rating. The policyholders are completely free to convert their existing term insurance into permanent insurance. If they can do this that policyholders of the company can expect to collect around $1.85 billion by the end of the year. We should take a look at deciding whether to invest in these companies.

Be sure to learn about the various policies that are available. Education is you the most. Like Koffi Anan has said, knowledge is power. It's essential to know which life insurance plan you need, which business to work with as well as their terms of compensation. You will be able to make informed choices for your family members, and other beneficiaries. Make a well-informed choice by utilizing your knowledge. Additionally, you should learn how to contact your appropriate personnel when it is necessary.

Health Insurance

Chapter 15: What Is Health Insurance?

Health Insurance is about quality of life. The term "quality life" is an inclusive term used to refer to a lifestyle that has an appropriate balance between the mental, physical as well as mental wellbeing of the person in question. The health of your body is an essential requirement to enjoy an enjoyable living. Maintain and enhance your health by taking medical insurance.

The health insurance you have is similar as obtaining a high-quality life insurance. This is an unspoken truth that is openly promoted and you are open to similar benefits? Alexis Carell carefully articulated this by stating"quality of life is more important than "quality of life is more important than life itself".

For you to be able to improve the quality of your life, and to reap the benefits as you age, look into the benefits of health insurance. This article explains the importance of health insurance and who can benefit from it, the best way to avail this coverage as well as the reason we require it.

Are we in need of Health Insurance, and at what Cost?

In the USA Health insurance in the US has been the subject of debate on television, as well as other social media sites. Many have been written on the subject and much more remains to be spoken about, specifically following this debate. In recent times, a trend is being discussed via social media. People are speaking out to the government in question regarding the effectiveness, rate and the necessity of healthcare insurance.

The public is complaining about the health systems that have been hampered by corruption and serve the interests of corporations, not the people. in 2021 Johonniuss Chemweno identified the gaps that were hindering the provision of healthcare to citizens of the country. Health care cost has been increasing exponentially over time this is detrimental to individuals and families who cannot pay for their medical bills.

What is Health Insurance Cover?

Health insurance will cover expenses of hospitalization in the event that a policyholder is ill. It will cover all illnesses as long as we've listed that they are among the covered perils. In the wake of the pandemic covid-19 the world has seen the erratic nature of life. It is possible to be completely wiped out one moment and be fighting to live the next. There is no doubt that you could provide at minimum two occasions where the world has exposed it's "cruel and unfair" side. In the year 2020, the amount of individuals who took out life insurance coverage shot up because health insurance doesn't pay an amount for death benefits.

Although we may say"better late than never however, I believe that the sooner we get started creating a plan for a good life and the more advantageous it will be for us and our families. Everyone deserves a quality life. It is a shame that we work so difficult to be able to give ourselves the very best living. That should be the goal and our motivation each moment. In the past, our grandparents had no health insurance plans. Today, we are able to enjoy cheap and flexible health insurance plans. Why are you still waiting? Grab this chance and protect your family's life as well as your own.

The increasing frequency of inherited and lifestyle illnesses, genetic illnesses, as well as the spread of pandemics, which is getting more and more each day, we must review our lifestyle choices and take informed decisions regarding our health as well as the people we love. Health insurance companies are going further to tailor their policies to meet the most prevalent health risks as well as those who live in the unpredictable seasons.

Dental Insurance covers dental treatment cost for its policyholders. In the USA and in other advanced countries the insurance is well-established coverage. Certain might seem a little extravagant however I can assure you that the cost of dental care could be astronomical.

As with other insurance policy, insurance for health plans can be purchased through brokers, insurance agent, or directly through the insurance company. The purchase of health insurance isn't a single-point process. It is necessary to research your options to assess your needs for health insurance, and compare various health insurance plans. Selecting the best health insurance firm as well as analyzing your needs for health insurance in the near future in conjunction with the settlement records will provide the best advice on making your selection based on your own preference.

Each journey starts with one step. Health insurance can be a breeze or a slow process, according to the path you take through the process of acquiring it. "Enjoying the fruits" has been deemed to be the most exciting portion of your insurance experience. Imagine visiting your preferred health center and receiving top-quality as well as affordable care without digging in your pockets to pay even a penny! That must be great! All of us deserve this kind of benefits to our health.

Why do I require Health Insurance?

Health insurance benefits are immediate and lifesaving. Insurance coverage for health comes to the rescue in case unexpected health issues. The effects of health problems, and particularly emergencies are financially draining. Health insurance is a way to prepare for these emergencies, and then can help plan your budget ahead. This is the essence of what quality living is all about.

Insurance coverage for health can provide you with the freedom to go into the hospital whenever you feel suitable. The coverage covers medical check-ups or consultations as well as any other hospital visits covered by the insurance plan. This means you are very conscious of taking care of your health.

The cost of health insurance' is not solely yours to bear, it will be shared by your employer and to the government. The majority of employers have to channel employee's monthly income into the health savings accounts of their employees. This is an advantage for employees. It is deducted from the employee prior to the funds are transferred into their accounts. It's a good idea to check that you do not fall behind on making payments for health insurance.

The U.S. government has been leading the way in ensuring that citizens have access to high-quality and cost-effective health care. A recent, well-known federal program can be described as Universal Healthcare Coverage (UHC).

Final Thoughts On Health Insurance

There is a lot we can talk about in regards to the quality of our lives, however, it's only a concept until you make the decision to act. John C. Maxwell says that "our decisions, not our conditions, determine our quality of life". Your commitment and accountability will allow you to achieve the quality of your life you desire.

Everyone should have coverage for health. It's never too late for people who don't possess health insurance. Just a few steps away of living a life without health or financial burdens. Choose today and protect your future as well as the one of your loved ones.

Homeowners Insurance

What is Homeowners Insurance?

Insurance for homes protects against damage to the home of a homeowner as well as other possessions within, as well as property damage.

Who is in need of Homeowners Insurance?

The idea of homeowner's insurance may sound as if it's a luxury for many, but you shouldn't become one of them. It is important to realize that insuring your house is essential. Imagine the mess that would be created by the time you return home to find clothing missing or most loved shoes damaged. To protect such properties, there's an obligation to have homeowners insurance.

It is possible that you don't own an apartment at the moment however there's something that you must know. A lot of landlords require tenants to keep Renters Insurance. Although it may not be important to you, however it's a requirement for landlords.

What is the best time to get Renter's or Homeowner's Insurance?

When you enter into a purchase contract for an apartment It's best to look into homeowners insurance. This gives you the an opportunity to have your policy put in place prior to closing the deal and allows you to review estimates from different insurance firms.

It is typical to have one month to go between the day you sign a contract until the time your new home will be closed. Do you need homeowner's insurance prior to closing? When you close, you'll usually require evidence to prove that you've already paid the homeowners' insurance premiums for the first entire year.

If the landlord you work for or your firm that handles property has a requirement for tenants to be insured as renters and you wish to take out the necessary insurance. So that you can reduce the risk that tenants could sue in the event of damage to their personal belongings or for liability charges The landlord may also require renter's insurance.

Chapter 16: What Exactly Does Home Insurance Cover?

The insurance coverage for your home covers four kinds of incidents including: exterior, inside and outside, damage or loss to personal items, and accidents that occur in the property insured. In the event of these incidents homeowners pay an amount for deductibles, while the insurance company pays the remainder, in case you bought an insurance policy that covers replacement costs.

Interior and Exterior Damage

Insurance companies pay an amount of compensation to your property if it suffers destruction from hurricanes, fires and vandalism. or other covered disasters and allows you to fix or completely rebuild your house. With regard to the policy you must be aware that catastrophes such as flooding, earthquakes, or inadequate property are not covered. If you require this type of protection you should consider adding additional riders. When you go to a homeowner's insurance provider, they'll remind you of the fact that the same regulations are applicable to garages, sheds or any other building that is located on your property. In this instance it is necessary to have an additional insurance policy.

Insurance for your home covers items like clothes, appliances and furniture in the event of results in damage. A coverage for off-premises of a homeowner's insurance policy lets you file claims for property that has been lost such as jewels. Most insurance companies provide a limit between 50% and 70 percent of the insurance coverage that you can get in the building of your house as per the Insurance Information Institute. If, for instance, the home is insured at the sum of $200,000, your possessions are covered up to $140,000.

You may have lots of high-end possessions, like fine art, antiques, fine jewelry or designer clothes. If that's the scenario, you might want for an additional sum of money for them to be listed in an organized schedule, or purchase a brand updated policy from the business.

The possibility of personal liability for damages or injuries to property somebody sues you for damages, the liability insurance policy will cover your rights. It also covers pets. If your pet bites Maggy or a neighbour the insurance policy will take care of any medical bills incurred by the incident occurs in your house or at her. You can also file an insurance claim for reimbursement when your dog damages the flower vase. In the same way, as when someone was injured at your home and you're covered in the event that Maggy gets her hands on broken vase and then sues you for pain or loss of revenue.

Based on the Insurance Information Institute, policies may provide just 100,000 in insurance, however experts suggest having at minimum 300,000. If you purchase an umbrella insurance policy, you could get an additional 1 million or more in protection at a cost of one hundred dollars annually.

Hotel reservations or your home during the construction or repair of your Home

While it's likely you'll need to leave your home for a short period of time it is undoubtedly the greatest Insurance you've ever purchased. If you experience any loss that is covered, your insurance policy will pay the cost of your hotel room, rent as well as dining out and any other costs. While you're waiting for your home to be habitable again.

When you are sitting in your hotel room and enjoy the benefits, make sure you take care to be moderate since some hotels impose limitations on booking suites and booking room services. Learn what the insurance policy allows and pay with this.

Why Do I Need Home Insurance?

There are many legitimate reasons to have a homeowner's insurance policy.

Protects Mortgage Investment

If you have your home by yourself, there's no need to carry homeowners' insurance. However, for mortgage lenders to accept to purchase your home the home must be covered by insurance. If a tornado, fire or lightning strike your property, it's straightforward to obtain repairs that protect the lender's investment.

Safeguards Your Home Structure

A homeowner's insurance policy's primary purpose is to secure the principal asset you have invested in. If you were to suffer an natural catastrophe such as the occurrence of a hurricane, your home would lose a substantial amount without homeowners' insurance.

It's recommended to get complete value protection for your house. However, it is also common to carry protection between 80% and 90 percent. Homeowner's Insurance generally will cover substantial, moderate as well as complete repair costs.

Protects the contents of your house

It is possible to add additional coverages to protect your personal belongings in the home, which includes important furniture, electronics as well as home appliances. Be sure to record all the items inside your home prior to buying a homeowner's insurance policy. Insurance policies can provide either a partial or full amount of compensation in the event that a damaged by a covered disaster or if it destroys certain belongings such as a hurricane.

Protection against natural catastrophes.

Natural disasters could make homeowners suffer huge expenses. Repairing a damaged house could take a large chunk of your savings and create a massive gap in your pocket. The insurance policy will protect you from loss caused by natural catastrophes when you purchase the complete insurance for your house. These insurance policy riders typically provides reimbursement in the event of catastrophes such as floods, landslides, or earthquakes of a monthly or annually scheduled price.

Protection of Separated Buildings.

The home you live in isn't the only thing covered under homeowners' insurance. They also cover adjacent spaces such as your deck the garage and even your fence. The insurer covers unattached structures at least 10% of their coverage. It is possible to alter the policy in case you require more protection for the unattached structure of your home.

Where Do I Buy Home Insurance?

Before you enter the market for insurance on your home it is important to consider the total cost of replacement for your home and the risk it's most susceptible to as well as the insurance costs you're able to pay.

After you've decided on the amount of insurance you'll need, examine rates from various insurance companies to find which one offers the most favorable rates. Look for a service that provides affordable prices, security features as well as a superior level of customer service.

A look at these firms could be an excellent first step when searching for insurance coverage for your home. These companies can also give you an idea of the things to consider when you make your decision.

Lemonade

Lemonade insurance is a simple way to get quotes and submit claims. The insurance company operates on the internet and employs artificial intelligence in order to provide rapid estimates and claims payments. All you have to do is go on their site and fill in a form that you can then select the type of coverage that you want.

Hippo

Hippo is the best choice for those who have a high-tech home due to its use of technology for greater security of your home as well as customer support. According to Hippo, Hippo enables customers to take advantage of the online quote system and get a quote in one minute and get an insurance policy in just five minutes. Hippo is also able to offer you. discounts on smart home. The discount only applies when you have create and accept to make use of a free smart home surveillance system.

Erie

Erie will cover replacement costs within its policy. It is an excellent assurance package that customers can avail. The company is ranked within the top 5 of its categories and is among the top insurance firms with regard to customer service and satisfaction. It also provides coverage for roofing damage, which is not the case with many other homeowners' insurance providers.

State Farm

State Farm is one of the largest insurance companies that cater to homeowners. But, if you're looking to get numerous discounts from your insurance company, it is possible to search elsewhere. State Farm offers few discounts. Discounts on multi-policy policies and security systems are included in the policy.

Amica Mutual

Amica Mutual offers the best customer care. The other thing you'll discover appealing about this business is the fact that their contractor database allows you to receive all the help required. Amica Mutual distinguishes itself for client service regarding coverage issues.

Chapter 17: Why Do I Require Renter's Insurance?

If buying a home isn't your top priority to you, understanding renter's insurance is crucial. Renters' Insurance adds endorsements and floaters that provide protection for personal belongings, the same like homeowners' insurance. Jewellery, devices and collections of other kinds, such as baseball cards, are some of the common items covered under the insurance policy.

If you are a tenant, you feel secure knowing your rental property is secured and secured by liability insurance as well as personal property insurance, wherever you travel.

How Much Renters Insurance Do I Need?

The renter's insurance that you purchase must be proportional to the value of your belongings in addition to any equipment or furniture provided by your landlord.. Another option is to get insurance with a higher value over the amount of things in the home that you are leasing. In the event that something happens to you and your home has been damaged, the right amount of insurance will safeguard you.

But, it is possible to purchase insurance that is less than the value of your belongings, if you want to risk the potential danger associated with this choice. If you are looking to cut costs on the policy should consider this option. If this is the route you're looking to follow be aware that the insurance provider provides coverage to a set amount of limits in the event of catastrophe.

Car / Auto Insurance

What is Auto Insurance?

If you are the owner of a car then you are well aware in protecting your car. If you are planning to own an insurance policy at some point in your life, it is important be aware of the reasons why it's essential to ensure that your vehicle is in good condition. The insurance policy will give you security should you be involved in an accident or the vehicle is vandalized or lost or damaged by an natural catastrophe.

People make semi-annual or annual payment to an insurance firm instead of having to pay the costs of auto accidents from their own the pocket. The company is then able to pay some or all of the expenses for the car damage.

If you decide to purchase insurance for your car it is essentially signing in a binding contract with the insurer, agreeing to cover premiums to protect yourself from financial loss caused by accidents, or any other harm to the car.

What are the main components of Auto Insurance?

Auto and car insurance policies comprise specific elements, each of which covers the same liability, and consequently decrease the risk.

Body Injury Coverage

If you, as the owner of the policy are liable for injuries to another person your injury, it will be covered under the personal injury insurance policy. If you are using the vehicle of someone else in their presence, they are insured along with any relatives listed in the policy.

It's essential to purchase sufficient liability insurance as should a catastrophe occur the risk of the possibility of a substantial financial claim. It's advisable for those who have insurance to purchase more liability insurance beyond the amount that is required by the government. The additional insurance protects your money and assets such as your house.

Own Damage Coverage

The coverage for own-damage, which is a vital element of comprehensive insurance for cars provides protection from any harm to the vehicle. The entire Information on own harm is provided in this section of the policy. It is helpful if you determine if the event which damaged your vehicle will be covered before filing an insurance claim.

Collision Coverage

Car damage caused by collisions with other vehicles or objects such as telephone poles, trees, or even flipping over is covered under collision insurance (note that deer-related collisions are protected under extensive coverage). Also, the damage caused by potholes is also covered.

In general, collision insurance is offered with the option of a separate the deductible. If you were to be the cause of the accident, your collision insurance would cover repair to your car and the associated deductible. If the incident occurred without fault on your part the insurance company could try to get reimbursement by contacting the insurer. If successful the insurance company will be able to pay for the cost of the deductible. If the vehicle you own is old and isn't worth much it is possible to consider removing the collision insurance.

Comprehensive Coverage

By taking out this insurance You are reimbursed in the event of losses caused by loss or damage resulting from causes that are not collisions with vehicle or object. Comprehensive events are collisions between birds or deer, fires, falling objects, missiles, storms, explosions, earthquakes flooding, hail vandalism, riots, and floods. If your windshield is damaged or cracked, it could also be advantageous to get it replaced.

While some insurance companies may offer the glass component of the policy for free however, you must purchase the full

Insurance that comes with the deductible that is separate.

Uninsured and Under-insured Drivers Coverage

It is possible to be struck with an uninsured driver, or one who's insurance does not fully cover the damage. If that happens you'll receive compensation through the coverage for underinsured motorists.

The coverage can also provide protection should you be involved in an accident that involves an insured driver, or when you are injured by an uninsured, or uninsured motorist while biking or walking.

How to Read an Auto Insurance Quote?

The insurance company guarantees to compensate you for loss according to the terms of the policy, with a amount. Policies that are individually priced allow customers to adjust the degree of coverage for your unique needs and financial limitations. The policies typically are renewed every either six or twelve months. In the event that it is the time to pay a new fee and to renew the policy insurance company will inform the consumer.

The majority of states require vehicle owners to have the bodily injury liability insurance which pays for the death or injuries caused by you or a driver creates while driving your car regardless of whether they insist on having a minimum amount of insurance for autos. Furthermore, they might need property damage liability which covers damage that either you or the driver of the vehicle that causes damage to other vehicles or pieces of property.

The amount of coverage (your insurance limit) that insurance companies will reimburse you for a covered incident, as well as the out-of-pocket costs in the event that you have to claim the benefits, will be included in your quotations for insurance.

Why do Different Deductible Amounts Affect Price so Much?

Health, property, and casualty insurance policies come with insurance the possibility of deductibles. Deductibles cover out-of-pocket costs prior to the time that the policy becomes effective and starts to pay out insurance claims.

The deductibles will vary based on the insurance company, the coverage as well as the amount of premium you have to are required to pay. It is a common practice that you will pay less prices for monthly or annually in the event of an excessive deductible. The reason for this is that there are a variety of expenses to pay prior to the coverage beginning. However anticipate higher premiums and less deductions. In this case the insurance company begins getting paid much more rapidly.

If policyholders make claim, insurers may split the costs since the policyholder pays the cost of deductibles. There are two conditions when it comes to deductibles: moral hazard as well as financial stability.

#1. Deductibles lower moral hazard risk

The risk that an insured could not behave in a honest manner is a moral risk. The insurance policy protects the insured against financial losses. Hence it is a moral risk: The insured can act freely and in a risky manner without having to worry about the financial risks.

In particular, those with insurance for their automobiles may be enticed to take care when driving. A deductible does not mean that they are in no say in what happens. As the insured is liable to certain expenses the deductible reduces that chance.

#2 Deductibles to ensure financial stability

Through reducing the amount of claim Insurance policies employ deductibles in order to provide financial stability for the insurance company's side. The right insurance plan will provide the protection against catastrophic losses. Deductibles are a cushion between a small and devastating loss.

Who Needs Car Insurance?

Most states will require drivers to carry auto insurance. But, it is not the case in certain states. Drivers who reside in New Hampshire are not required to have auto insurance. However, they must show proof of their capacity to pay for any costs incurred by any accident that is their duty.

As the law mandates that most drivers have insurance. It doesn't suggest that you must only have only the minimum amount of insurance.

When Should I buy Car Insurance?

The ownership of a vehicle has been considered to be a sign of freedom and unlimited opportunities. The feeling is that you're cranking up the volume and speeding across the horizon in a dazzling color. The first sequence of music is played. Car ownership is a blessing with helpful advice to take advantage of the thrilling excursions you plan to embark with your car: good driving is accompanied by a significant financial burden.

If you're wondering if you require insurance for your car before purchasing your vehicle The answer is yes. It is not necessary to purchase an insurance policy to bring your baby to home. The majority of women think of cars as their babies today. There is no need to buy Insurance however I doubt you'd like to go that route.

The likelihood is that you won't be legally able to leave with your latest purchase if you do not have Insurance. In certain states, registration procedures typically begin with the dealer, and the majority of states require confirmation that liability insurance is in place. Although it's not mandatory to have auto insurance, it's generally a smart idea prior to purchasing a vehicle.

Chapter 18: Where Do I Buy Car Insurance?

Insurance for cars may be offered from the dealership. The lender, for instance might be willing to arrange insurance to you when you finance your car through the dealer and must have insurance for collision as well as comprehensive. While it might seem like a good idea however, it isn't the most effective method of finding the cheapest price for car insurance.

The dealer or lender could only work with a couple of insurance companies. It is possible to research and evaluate rates of various insurance companies before you shop. This will help you save the time and expense of asking for quotes from the dealer.

When you are a teen, it is possible that you will want the same insurer that your parents do. Be aware that your parents could have had their insurance through the same company for a number of years, and thus receive excellent discounts for drivers, however it's not a guarantee that this is the right choice for you.

The most effective method is to look at prices of different companies. In this article, I'll highlight few of the reviews on the best insurance companies that you can work with. These include:

Nationwide

For certain types of drivers, as well as other add-on insurance coverages Nationwide provides reasonable rates on automobile insurance. This is an insurance company worth considering if seeking auto insurance since there are a lot of complaints about the coverage it offers is quite minimal. Nationwide allows drivers to reduce their premiums according to actual usage using a usage-based plan of insurance with a pay per mile choice.

Travelers

Overall, Travelers has an affordable price for a range of motorists. It is a great choice to think about when looking at comparison buying because it offers numerous additional options to offer you superior insurance coverage. There are very few complaints from insurance companies of state.

State Farm

You should think about State Farm due to its extremely competitive rates for auto insurance and its lower complaint rate. State Farm is among the most reliable companies to deal with especially when you've caused an accident in the past. If you're seeking reductions while they are watching you closely, State Farm is the most suitable option. But if you're searching for a brand new car I suggest you shop other places.

Allstate

Allstate offers a broad range of insurance options, including deductibles that disappear to forgiveness. Additionally, the company has a the distinction of having a low number of claims against its vehicle insurance submitted to state insurance departments that helps to balance out the rates that are often more expensive than its most reputable competitors.

Erie Insurance

Erie provides solid coverage and is rated highly in handling claims for repair of accidents. The benefits are balanced by Erie's fluctuating car insurance rates based on your driving habits.

www.ingramcontent.com/pod-product-compliance
Lightning Source LLC
Chambersburg PA
CBHW070556010526
44118CB00012B/1334